Advances in Project Management

Advances in Project Management

Narrated Journeys in Unchartered Territory

Edited by

DARREN DALCHER
National Centre for Project Management

Published by
Gower Publishing Limited
Wey Court East
Union Road
Farnham
Surrey, GU9 7PT
England

Gower Publishing Company
110 Cherry Street
Suite 3-1
Burlington, VT 05401-3818
USA

www.gowerpublishing.com

British Library Cataloguing in Publication Data
A catalogue record for this book is available from the British Library

ISBN: 9781472429124 (hbk)
ISBN: 9781472429131 (ebk – ePDF)
ISBN: 9781472429148 (ebk – ePUB)

Library of Congress Cataloging-in-Publication Data
Dalcher, Darren.
  Advances in project management : narrated journeys in unchartered territory / by Darren Dalcher, [chief contributor and editor].
    pages cm. – (Advances in project management)
  Includes bibliographical references and index.
  ISBN 978-1-4724-2912-4 (hardback) – ISBN 978-1-4724-2913-1 (ebook) 1. Project management.
I. Title.
  HD69.P75D348 2014
  658.4'04–dc23
                                                                                      2013035197

Printed in the United Kingdom by Henry Ling Limited,
at the Dorset Press, Dorchester, DT1 1HD

Contents

List of Figures and Tables   *ix*

About the Editor   *xi*

Notes on Contributors   *xiii*

Introduction   1

1   Uncertainty
Managing Project Uncertainty   7
Darren Dalcher

    That Uncertain Feeling   9
    David Cleden

2   Strategic Risk
When do Projects Begin? Addressing Strategic Project
Appraisal Issues   15
Darren Dalcher

    Strategic Project Risk Appraisal and Management   17
    Elaine Harris

3   Risk
Risks or Projects?   23
Darren Dalcher

    Managing Risk in Projects: What's New?   27
    David Hillson

4   Governance
Facing Uncertainty: Project Governance and Control   31
Darren Dalcher

    Project Governance   33
    Ralf Müller

5 Programme Management
Managing Uncertainty through Programmes 39
Darren Dalcher

Programme Management beyond Standards and Guides 41
Michel Thiry

6 Risk Leadership
Beyond Tame Problems: The Case for Risk Leadership 49
Darren Dalcher

The Application of the 'New Sciences' to Risk and Project Management 51
David Hancock

7 Leadership
In Search of Project Leadership 57
Darren Dalcher

Project-oriented Leadership 59
Ralf Müller and Rodney Turner

8 Earned Value
Progress and Performance: The Case for Extending Earned Value Management 63
Darren Dalcher

Effective Measurement of Time Performance using Earned Value Management 67
Alexandre Rodrigues

9 Spiritual Inspiration
Inspiration in Teams: Searching for a New Intelligence 97
Darren Dalcher

Spirituality in Project Management Teams 99
Judi Neal and Alan Harpham

10 Ethics
Project Ethics and Professionalism: The Making of a Profession? 107
Darren Dalcher

Project Ethics: The Critical Path to Development 109
Haukur Ingi Jónasson and Helgi Thor Ingason

11 Stakeholders
Can We Satisfy Project Stakeholders?   113
Darren Dalcher

What Does the Project Stakeholder Value?   115
Pernille Eskerod and Anna Lund Jepsen

12 Supply Chains
Managing Connected Supply Chains   119
Darren Dalcher

Managing Project Supply Chains   121
Ron Basu

13 Second Order Project Management
Making Sense of Complexity: Towards a Higher Order   127
Darren Dalcher

A Case for Second Order Project Management   129
Michael Cavanagh

14 Sustainability
Sustainability: A New Professional Responsibility?   135
Darren Dalcher

**Taking Responsibility: The Integration of Sustainability
and Project Management**   137
Gilbert Silvius and Ron Schipper

15 Psychology
The Psychology of Projects: What the Bodies of Knowledge
Don't Tell Us   145
Darren Dalcher

The Psychology of Project Management   149
Sharon De Mascia

16 Benefits
Overstating the Benefits?   155
Darren Dalcher

**Benefits Realisation – Building on (un)Safe Foundations
or Planning for Success?**   157
Stephen Jenner

17 **The Burden of Making Good Decisions** 165
Darren Dalcher

Decision Making under Stress – Advice for Project Leaders 169
Kaye Remington

18 **Leadership Communication**
The Art of Communication 179
Darren Dalcher

Communicating Upwards for Effect 183
Lynda Bourne

19 **Sustainable Impacts**
Sustainability and Success 187
Darren Dalcher

Sustainable Change in Large Projects 191
Göran Brulin and Lennart Svensson

20 **Knowledge**
Is There a Universal Theory of Project Management? 197
Darren Dalcher

The Coming Sea-Change in Project Management Science 201
Michael Hatfield

21 **Senior Management**
From Projects to Strategy, and Back Again 207
Darren Dalcher

**Evidence of the Neglect of Project Management
by Senior Executives** 211
Antonio Nieto-Rodriguez

Summary – Project Management Research: The Long Journey 221

Index 225

List of Figures and Tables

Figures

1.1	The illusion of project stability	10
1.2	Four possible modes for confronting uncertainty	12
1.3	Making an intuitive leap to visualise a future scenario	13
2.1	IT project risk map	19
4.1	Four project governance paradigms	35
4.2	Framework for governance of project, programme and portfolio management	36
4.3	Model of project governance	38
5.1	The mature programme integration	42
5.2	The programme decision management cycle	44
5.3	The programme life cycle	46
8.1	The relationship between project scope, cost and time elements	69
8.2	Planned value	69
8.3	Earned value	70
8.4	Resource consumption	70
8.5	The late finish problem	74
8.6	The early finish problem	76
8.7	Earned schedule	79
8.8	The final value for SPI(t)	81
8.9	Conventional SPI compared to SPI(t)	83
8.10	The behaviour of SPI(t) in the case of a late finish	88
8.11	The behaviour of SPI(m) in the case of an early finish	91
12.1	Project supply chain building blocks	123
17.1	Hebb's version of the Yerkes–Dodson Principle	170
17.2	Original Yerkes–Dodson Principle	171

Tables

2.1	Project risk attributes for business development projects	19
2.2	Mitigating actions	20
6.1	The new concept of risk leadership	56
7.1	Competences and their measurement	60
7.2	Hierarchy of importance of specific leadership competencies by project type	60
8.1	Figures for the scenario	89
8.2	An extended EVM model for time management using the modified SPI	92
14.1	The contrast between the concepts of sustainable development and project management	140
16.1	Five of the main cognitive biases and their impact on benefits forecasting	158
21.1	Project management as a discipline in top business schools	216
21.2	Number of references/articles per topic, *Harvard Business Review* (3 July 2011)	218

About the Editor

Professor Darren Dalcher PhD (Lond) HonFAPM FRSA FBCS CITP FCMI is Professor of Project Management at the University of Hertfordshire, Visiting Professor at the University of Iceland and Adjunct Professor at the Lille Graduate School of Management (SKEMA). He is the Founder and Director of the National Centre for Project Management (NCPM), an interdisciplinary centre of excellence operating in collaboration with industry, government, charities, non-government organisations (NGOs) and the learned societies. The centre aims to set the national agenda and establish project management as a major profession and discipline in the UK. The centre is thus concerned with fostering active dialogue about the integration of successful practice and theoretical research within project management.

Following industrial and consultancy experience in managing technology projects, Professor Dalcher gained his PhD from King's College, University of London. In 1992, he founded an Institute of Electrical and Electronics Engineers (IEEE) taskforce focused on learning from project failures. He is active in numerous international committees, standards bodies, steering groups and editorial boards. He is heavily involved in organising international conferences, and has delivered many international keynote addresses and tutorials. He has written over 150 refereed papers and book chapters on project management and software engineering. He is Editor-in-Chief of the *Journal of Software: Evolution and Process*. He is the editor of the *Advances in Project Management* book series published by Gower Publishing which synthesises leading-edge knowledge, skills, insights and reflections in project and programme management and of its companion series, *Fundamentals of Project Management*, which provides the essential grounding in key areas of project management.

He has built a reputation as leader and innovator in the area of practice-based education and reflection in project management and has worked with many major industrial, commercial and charitable organisations and government bodies. In 2008 he was named by the Association for Project Management (APM) as one of the top ten influential experts in project management and has also been voted *Project Magazine*'s Academic of the Year for his contribution to 'integrating and weaving academic work with practice'. He has been Chairman of the influential APM Project Management Conference since 2009, setting consecutive attendance records and bringing together the most influential speakers.

He received international recognition in 2009 with appointment as a member of the PMForum International Academic Advisory Council, which features leading academics from some of the world's top universities and academic institutions. The council showcases accomplished researchers, influential educators shaping the next generation of project managers and recognised authorities on modern project management. In October 2011 he was awarded a prestigious Honorary Fellowship from the APM for outstanding contributions to project management.

He has delivered lectures and courses in many international institutions, including King's College London, Cranfield Business School, ESC Lille, Iceland University, University of Southern Denmark and George Washington University. His research interests include project success and failure; maturity and capability; ethics; process improvement; agile project management; systems and software engineering; performance management; project benchmarking; risk management; decision making; chaos and complexity; project leadership; change management; knowledge management; and evidence-based and reflective practice.

Professor Dalcher is an Honorary Fellow of the APM, a Chartered Fellow of the British Computer Society, a Fellow of the Chartered Management Institute and the Royal Society of Arts, and a Member of the Project Management Institute, the Academy of Management, the Institute for Electrical and Electronics Engineers and the UK Systems Society. He is a Chartered IT Practitioner. He is a Member of the Project Management Institute (PMI) Advisory Board responsible for the prestigious David I. Cleland Project Management Award; of the APM Group Ethics and Standards Governance Board, and, until recently, of the APM Professional Development Board. He is an Academic and Editorial Advisory Council Member for *PM World Journal*, for which he also writes a regular column featuring advances in research and practice in project management.

Notes on Contributors

Ron Basu is Director of Performance Excellence Limited and a Visiting Fellow at Henley Business School, England. He specialises in operational excellence and supply chain management and has research interests in performance management and project management. Previously he held senior management roles in blue-chip companies like GSK, GlaxoWellcome and Unilever and led global initiatives and projects in Six Sigma, ERP/MRPII, supply chain re-engineering and total productive maintenance. Prior to this he worked as Management Consultant with A.T. Kearney. He is the co-author of *Total Manufacturing Solutions, Quality Beyond Six Sigma, Total Operations Solutions* and *Total Supply Chain Management* and the author of *Measuring e-Business Performance, Implementing Quality, Implementing Six Sigma and Lean, FIT SIGMA, Managing Project Supply Chains* and *Managing Project Quality*. He has authored a number of papers in the operational excellence and project management fields. He is a regular presenter of papers in global seminars on project management, Six Sigma, manufacturing and supply chain topics.

Lynda Bourne is Managing Director of Stakeholder Management Pty Ltd – an Australian-based company with partners in South America and Europe. Through this global network she works with organisations to manage change through managing the relationships essential for successful delivery of organisational outcomes. Lynda was the first graduate of the RMIT University, Doctor of Project Management course, where her research was focused on tools and techniques for more effective stakeholder engagement. She has been recognised in the field of project management through her work on development of project and programme management standards. She was also included in Project Management Institute's (PMI) list of the 50 most influential women in project management. She is a Fellow of the Australian Institute of Management (AIM) and a Fellow of the Australian Computer Society (ACS). She is a recognised international speaker and seminar leader on the topic of stakeholder management, the Stakeholder Circle® visualisation tool, and building credibility and reputation for more effective communication. She has extensive experience as a senior project manager and project director specialising in delivery of information technology (IT) and other business-related projects within the telecommunications sector, working as a senior IT project management consultant with various telecommunications companies in Australia and South East Asia (primarily in Malaysia) including senior roles with Optus and Telstra. Lynda's publications include *Stakeholder Relationship Management*, now in its second edition (2009), and *Advising Upwards* (2011).

Göran Brulin is senior analyst at the Swedish Agency for Economic and Regional Growth. He is responsible for the ongoing evaluation of the European Regional Development Programmes. He is Adjunct Professor in Local and Regional Innovations at Linköping University and associated with HELIX VINN, Centre of Excellence (see www.liu.se/helix). His research interests include interactive local and regional development, organisation of work, business administration and management, and economic sociology.

Michael Cavanagh has worked as a programmer, systems analyst, project manager, department head and consultant in a number of business sectors over his 45-year career. An independent management consultant and conference speaker since 1991, his earlier specialisations were in the fields of project management and the risk and ethical implications of technology, particularly with regard to safety-critical and safety-related systems design in software-intensive systems. He is now concentrating on more in-depth research into ethical issues in complex engineering projects and has recently published an eBook on the subject. Michael is also an ordained Anglican priest in the Church of Ireland and is currently responsible for the churches of the Kenmare and Dromod Union, Co. Kerry.

David Cleden is a senior project manager, bid writer and consultant with more than 25 years' experience in the public services IT sector. In addition to writing bids and successfully delivering complex projects for a wide range of commercial clients, he writes widely on a variety of business-related issues. David's first book, *Managing Project Uncertainty*, was the initial title in the Gower series on Advances in Project Management. His second book, *Bid Writing for Project Managers* has also been published by Gower.

Sharon De Mascia is the Director of 'Cognoscenti' (Chartered Business Psychologists). She has extensive project management experience and is PRINCE2 qualified. Sharon has 25 years of experience in delivering change management and other organisational initiatives across both public and private sectors. In the past she has worked with the NHS, The Employment Service, The Highways Agency, The Cooperative Insurance Society, Vita Group and Mendas. Sharon is a supervisor for the global MBA at Manchester Business School and a guest lecturer at Liverpool John Moores University in the UK. She is an assessor for the British Psychological Society and the Health Professions Council and an examiner for the International Baccalaureate in Psychology.

Pernille Eskerod is Professor in Project Management at the University of Southern Denmark. Pernille has almost 20 years of experience in research and teaching within project management. She has carried out a number of in-depth case studies. Pernille has published several journal articles and book chapters within project management, and is a well-known speaker at international conferences. Pernille is co-author of *Project Stakeholder Management* published by Gower Publishing as, part of the Advances in Project Management series edited by Professor Darren Dalcher.

David Hancock is Head of Project Risk for London Underground part of Transport for London. He has a wide breadth of knowledge in project management and complex projects and extensive experience in opportunity and risk management, with special regard to the people and behavioural aspects. Trained in the use of psychometrics, he has used this to produce high performing teams and bring innovation and creativity into projects. He champions the case for rethinking project management as a social interaction rather than delivery through the application of process and developed the concept of Risk Leadership. From 1998–2001 he was responsible for creating and delivering the Opportunity–Risk management system for the successful £4.2bn Terminal 5 Project at Heathrow, working with British Airways (BA), British Airports Authority (BAA) and their suppliers – which is considered industry leading in project and opportunity/risk management. Before that he spent ten years in REME (Royal Electrical and Mechanical Engineers) with the Army and the Royal Marines on duty around the globe in support of helicopter operations. He has spoken and lectured across Europe, Asia, Africa and North and South America. He was educated at the University of Nottingham where he obtained a degree and a PhD in engineering and later added an MBA from the University of Bath and a political and social science qualification from the University of Oxford. He is a Chartered Engineer and a Chartered Fellow of the Institute of Personnel and Development and was the public sector risk manager of the year in 2008.

Alan Harpham describes himself as being on his fourth career as what Charles Handy calls 'a portfolio manager'. Alan is the Chairman of the Association for Project Management Group (APMG), a global accreditation, registration and examination certification body for key elements of best practice in programme and project management. He is also a non-executive director with Subject Matters, a consultancy specialising in organising business-to-business events, conferences and exhibitions. He was a founding director of P5 – the Power of Projects, a consultancy specialising in the application of project and programme management in owner/client organisations. He started his career as a civil engineer with John Laing and held various roles there including section engineer through to International M&E Contracts Manager. He is on the Jury of the International Project Management Association's (IPMA) International Project Management Award.

Elaine Harris is Professor of Accounting and Management and Director of the Business School at the University of Roehampton. She has over 25 years of experience in higher education. Prior to that Elaine worked in accountancy practice as an auditor, accountant, consultant and manager. Elaine's research is focused upon how managers make sense of risky business propositions and prospective projects, and how they interact with other organisation members and external parties in reaching strategic investment decisions. Elaine has carried out research funded by commercial enterprises such as Christian Salveson PLC (1999–2003) and professional bodies such as the Chartered Institute of Management Accountants (CIMA) (2004–2006). She is a member of the European Risk Research Network (funded by Marie Curie 2007–2009) and has been the current chair of the research network, the Management Control Association since 2010. She is the author of *Strategic Project Risk Appraisal and Management* published by Gower Publishing, part of the Advances in Project Management series edited by Professor Darren Dalcher.

Michael Hatfield is the author of *Game Theory in Management* (Gower Publishing, 2012) and *Things Your PMO Is Doing Wrong* (PMI, 2008), but is probably best known as the author of the long-running column in *PMNetwork* magazine, 'Variance Threshold'. Besides *PMNetwork*, his work has appeared in the *Project Management Journal*, *Cost Engineering*, *Gantthead*, *People on Projects*, *The Measurable News*, and even in the *Nuclear Weapons Journal*. He has worked as an entry-level technician for the Air Force Weapons Laboratory's Electro-Magnetic Pulse (EMP) test sites, as the director of a National Laboratory's Project Management Office overseeing a budget of $1.3 Billion (USD), and many very interesting jobs in-between.

David Hillson is internationally recognised as a leading thinker and practitioner in risk management. He is Director of Risk Doctor and Partners, and has worked in over 40 countries. He is a popular conference speaker and award-winning author on risk, with six books on the topic. David has made several innovative contributions to improving risk management and is well known for promoting the inclusion of proactive opportunity management within the risk process, and for his groundbreaking work in risk psychology. David is an Honorary Fellow of the UK Association for Project Management (APM) and past chairman of its Risk Management Specific Interest Group. He is an elected Fellow of the Institute of Risk Management (IRM), the Royal Society for the Encouragement of Arts, Manufactures and Commerce (RSA), and the UK Chartered Management Institute (CMI). David is also an active member of the PMI and was a founder member of its Risk Management Specific Interest Group. He received the PMI Distinguished Contribution Award for his work in developing risk management over many years. Since 1998 he has been a core author for the risk chapter of the *PMBOK Guide®*, and is a core author for the PMI Practice Standard for Project Risk Management.

Helgi Thor Ingason is an Associate Professor at Reykjavik University and lectures in project management, quality management and systems dynamics modelling. He is the head of the MPM – Master in Project Management – programme at the university. He is a co-founder and senior consultant at the Nordica Consulting Group in Iceland and co-founder and chairman of Alur, alvinnsla hf – a recycling company in the aluminium industry in Iceland. He is an IPMA Certified Senior Project Manager.

Stephen Jenner is co-author and Chief Examiner for 'Management of Portfolios' and was previously Director of the Criminal Justice Integrated Team (CJIT) where the approach adopted to portfolio and benefits management won the 2007 Civil Service Financial Management Award. He is a regular speaker at international conferences, and a trainer and writer on the subjects of portfolio and benefits management. He is the author of several books in the field and is a professionally qualified management accountant and a Fellow of the APM. Steve also holds an MBA and Masters of Studies degree from Cambridge University. Steve is currently working on new guidance on *'Managing Benefits'* which will form the basis for accredited examinations from the APMG.

Anna Lund Jepsen is Associate Professor in marketing at the University of Southern Denmark. In her research and teaching she mainly works within the field of consumer behaviour and research methodology. Anna has worked together with Pernille on a number of case studies within project management. Anna is co-author of *Project Stakeholder Management* which was published by Gower Publishing as part of the Advances in Project Management series edited by Professor Darren Dalcher.

Haukur Ingi Jónasson is currently a lecturer at Reykjavik University, a psychoanalyst in private practice and a management consultant at Nordica Consulting Group ehf. His consulting assignments have included clients such as Landsbankinn, SPRON bank, University of Iceland, B&L (Land Rover, Hyundai, BMW, Renault, Rolls Royce), The Icelandic Church Aid, Actavis, The Icelandic National Energy Authority, Reykjavik City, The Association of Social Workers in Iceland, The Federation of State and Municipal Employees, the University Hospital of Iceland, University of Iceland and others.

Ralf Müller is Professor of Business Administration at Umeå University, Sweden and Professor of Project Management at BI Norwegian Business School, Norway. He lectures and researches in governance and management of projects, as well as in research methodologies. He is the (co)author of more than 140 publications and received, among others, the *Project Management Journal's* 2009 Paper of the Year, 2009 IRNOP's best conference paper award, and several Emerald Literati Network Awards for outstanding journal papers and referee work. He holds an MBA degree from Heriot Watt University and a DBA degree from Henley Management College, Brunel University, UK. Before joining academia he spent 30 years in the industry consulting large enterprises and governments in 47 different countries for their project management and governance. He also held related line management positions, such as the Worldwide Director of Project Management at NCR Teradata.

Judi Neal is the Director of the Tyson Center for Faith and Spirituality in the Workplace at the Sam M. Walton College of Business, University of Arkansas, USA. She received her PhD from Yale University. In 1992 Judi made faith and spirituality in the workplace a central focus of her research and presentations, and has gained a reputation in the national media for stressing the importance and value of faith and spirituality into the workplace. She was the Founder of The International Center for Spirit at Work and the International Spirit at Work Awards. Judi authored *Edgewalkers: People and Organizations that Take Risks, Build Bridges and Break New Ground*. She helped to co-found the Management, Spirituality and Religion Interest Group at the Academy of Management, and was the group's second Chair. She is also a co-founder of the *Journal of Management, Spirituality, and Religion*. She is Professor Emeritus at the University of New Haven and Academic Director of the Master of Arts in Organizational Leadership Program at the Graduate Institute.

Antonio Nieto-Rodriguez is the Head of Transversal Portfolio Management and in charge of the entire portfolio and project management practices at BNP Paribas Fortis. In addition to being member of the board of the London Business School Alumni in Belgium, he also holds a membership with the PMI Belgium Chapter Board and was a founding member of the PMI EMEA Corporate Networking Group. Prior to becoming elected to the Board of Directors, Antonio was the Head of Post-merger Integration at Fortis Bank, leading what was the largest takeover in financial services history: the acquisition of ABN AMRO. Before that, he worked for ten years at PricewaterhouseCoopers as a senior manager, becoming the global lead practitioner for project management. He is the author of the book *The Focused Organization*, and has been featured in several magazines, including *PM Network®*, *Strategy Business Review* and *The Economist*. Antonio is a Professor of Project Management for MBA students at several business schools, and is a regular keynote speaker at large international events. As a hobby, Antonio teaches business students and convinces senior leaders about the value of project management, positioning project management as a key management concept for executing organisation's strategies.

Kaye Remington is author of *Leading Complex Projects* (Gower Publishing, 2010) and co-author of *Tools for Complex Projects* (Gower Publishing, 2007). With over 25 years of senior management and project experience she is also a former Director of the Post-graduate Project Management Program at the University of Technology, Sydney. Kaye now runs a small consulting firm that works internationally to help organisations to develop their capacity to deliver complex strategy and projects.

Alexandre Rodrigues regularly publishes articles in trade and scientific magazines, and is guest speaker at various national and international conferences. In 1996 he was co-organiser of a NATO Advanced Research Workshop on the theme 'Managing and Modelling Complex Projects', which took place in Kiev, Ukraine and brought together a range of international experts in this area. Besides his business activities, he amassed over a decade of teaching experience in universities, having taught and conducted courses in the area of Project Management and Master's Degrees in both Portuguese and British universities. He is a member of the PMI, and was founding president of its representation in Portugal, the PMI–Portugal Chapter. From 2003–2007 he was mentor of PMI Chapters for the European region.

Ron Schipper is Project Manager and Consultant at Van Aetsveld, a leading consulting firm in project and change management in the Netherlands. He has more than 15 years of experience as a project manager in realising (organisational) change in various organisations. Besides executing projects, he is interested in developing the profession of project managers and transferring this knowledge to other practitioners in Netherlands and developing countries. With sustainability as the emerging theme for the world, his interest in the implications for projects and project management and the development of the professional role of project managers has developed. Ron has published on the sustainability of organisational change and is a regular presenter on professional seminars and conferences. He is an assessor for the Dutch IPMA Project Excellence Award.

Gilbert Silvius is Professor at HU University of Applied Sciences Utrecht in the Netherlands and principal consultant at Van Aetsveld, specialising in project and change management. He is founder and programme director of the Master of Project Management programme at HU and an active member of IPMA, PMI and the ISO TC258.

Lennart Svensson is Professor in Sociology at Linköping University and a member of the research management team at HELIX VINN, Centre of Excellence. He is also Research Manager at APeL, a research and development (R&D) centre for workplace learning and the framework for different development projects. His research field has covered local and regional development, workplace learning, interactive research, networks, partnerships and project work. He is author or co-author of more than 30 books.

Michel Thiry has over 35 years of professional experience after graduating as an architect. Following a fruitful career in construction, he has now focused on combining his value, project and programme management expertise to organisational issues. He is recognised as a worldwide authority in strategic applications of project, programme and value. He has supported the development and implementation of a number of strategic programmes for large multinational organisations, including their restructuring as project-based organisations (PBO). For the last 15 years, Michel has provided his expertise to major organisations, in various fields, including construction, financial, pharmaceutical, IT and information systems (IS), telecoms, water treatment, transportation (air and rail), local government and others. He is a regular keynote speaker for major international events and seminar leader for PMI SeminarsWorld since 2001. He has written and lectured widely in international forums, both at the academic and practice levels. In addition to his book *Value Management Practice*, published by the PMI, he has written a number of book chapters on value, programme and portfolio management. In 2006 he was elected PMI Fellow for his continued contribution to project management and in 2007 he was nominated Fellow of the Association for Project Management. In 2008, he was awarded a Life Achievement Award by the Canadian Society of Value Analysis.

Rodney Turner is Professor of Project Management at the SKEMA Business School, in Lille, France. He is Visiting Professor at Henley Business School and the Kemmy Business School, Limerick, and Adjunct Professor at the University of Technology Sydney. Rodney is the author or editor of 16 books, including *The Handbook of Project-based Management*, the bestselling book published by McGraw-Hill, and the *Gower Handbook of Project Management*. He is editor of *The International Journal of Project Management*. He lectures on project management worldwide. Rodney is Vice President, Honorary Fellow and former Chairman of the UK's APM, and former President and Chairman of the IPMA. He is a member of the Institute of Directors and Fellow of the Institution of Mechanical Engineers.

The chapter contributions in this volume were published with the help of *PM World Journal*.

The *PM World Journal* (*PMWJ*) is an online publication produced by PM World Inc. in the United States, but created by a virtual team of advisors, correspondents and contributing editors located worldwide. Each month, the *PMWJ* features dozens of new articles, papers and stories about programmes, projects and project management (P/PM) around the world. Objectives for the journal are to (1) support the creation of new P/PM knowledge; (2) support the transfer of that knowledge to individuals, organisations and locations where professional P/PM may be weak, less available or sorely needed; (3) provide recognition and visibility for authors, the creators of new P/PM knowledge; (4) provide an easily accessible and useful online repository of P/PM knowledge and information as a global resource for knowledge sharing and continuous learning; and (5) promote the application of modern, professional P/PM for solving more of the world's problems – to make this world a better place.

Project management experts, leaders and practitioners are invited to submit an article, paper or story for publication in the *PMWJ*. Share knowledge, gain visibility and help change the world. Visit www.pmworldjournal.net or contact editor@pmworldjournal.net.

Introduction

The hardest part of starting a new journey is taking a leap of faith right at the beginning …

–Anon.

This book has emerged from the search for refining and redefining the boundaries of project management. While the topics may be briefly mentioned in the various standards and bodies of knowledge, the individual chapters are often reflections on new developments that stretch contemporary understanding, offering new insights and perspectives. In fact, a large proportion of the writing extends beyond widely recognised knowledge aspects to feature a much-needed focus on the skills, attitudes, values and competencies that are needed to successfully deliver projects.

In recent years we have also seen a plethora of new books and articles identifying the shortcomings of traditional methods and proposing alternative arrangements, solutions and conceptualisations. Many of these publications are initiated by practitioners who appear to be dissatisfied by the current state of affairs. Yet, given the range and diversity of such publications it is becoming increasingly difficult to sample, understand and identify all the contributions that may be applicable to us.

The chapters collated in this publication bring together many leading authorities on topics that are relevant to the management of projects. Topics such as sustainability, leadership, governance, programme management, decision making, problem solving, psychology, messy problems and ethics are explored alongside more traditional aspects such as risk, supply chains, earned value and performance measurement.

The main aims of the work are to reflect on the state of practice in the discipline; to offer some fresh insights and thinking; to distil new knowledge;

and, to provide a way of sampling a range of ideas, perspectives and styles of writing from some of the leading thinkers in the discipline.

The content is divided into 21 specific areas. In each area a brief introductory narrative that sets the context and explains the background is followed by a chapter focused on a particular aspect, approach or new way of thinking. Readers who might like to follow up the ideas are strongly encouraged to refer to the books published by the authors of the pertinent chapters which offer greater detail and significantly more content on the relevant topic.

Taken together the book offers both a unique distillation of ideas from a wide range of authors on many topics that extend beyond the bodies of knowledge, and an accessible introduction to further resources in the areas that they would like to explore. As the range of topics extends beyond those normally covered, it is likely that the book will identify new perspectives that readers may not have considered, and thereby suggest additional reading to augment the interests and concerns of practitioners and researchers.

Why Project Management?

Project management is increasingly being recognised as a key competence in many organisations in both the public and private sectors. Trends such as downsizing, reduced management layers, greater flexibility, distributed teams and the challenges of rapidly evolving technology have taken project management beyond its routes in the construction, engineering and aerospace industries and are playing a part in transforming the service, financial, IT and general management sectors. Academic courses, professional training and accreditation programmes are blossoming as practitioners seek to enhance their knowledge, skills and competencies. *Fortune* even rated project management as the number one career choice at the beginning of the twenty-first century.

Project management offers the discipline and framework required to help organisations to transform their mainstream operations and service performance. It is viewed as a way of organising for the future. Moreover, in an increasingly busy, stressful and uncertain world it has become necessary to manage multiple projects successfully at the same time.

Project management is a core competence required to deliver change measured in terms of achieving desired outcomes with associated benefits.

With projects increasingly viewed as managing the change efforts of society, project management is called upon to cross functional, organisational and societal boundaries and handle the inherent complexity and uncertainty required to bring about a new reality.

Yet, many organisations have struggled in applying the traditional models of project management to their new projects in the global environment. Projects still fail at an alarming rate. A major ingredient in the build-up leading to failure is often cited as the lack of adequate project management knowledge and experience.

Some organisations have responded to this situation by trying to improve the understanding and capability of their managers and employees who are introduced to projects, as well as their experienced project managers, in an attempt to enhance their competence and capability in this area.

Why Now?

There are many reasons why we need to refocus the discussion on improving the management of projects: modern organisations feature flatter structures, new technologies, rising complexity, greater collaboration and increasing interactions all requiring greater responsiveness. We also need vision and direction to drive our efforts.

The world of projects has changed dramatically. The old models appear less relevant and the dated tools less useful in context. Successful delivery in increasingly competitive and global environments require us to align with organisational strategy, focus on practitioners, and create the right environment to foster the skills and attitudes needed to succeed at the grand challenges facing us.

We seem to live in a faster and more demanding world, characterised by rising levels of uncertainty and ambiguity. Indeed, project management is increasingly called upon to deliver in a world that is connected in complex new ways; where the so-called 'unknown unknowns' determine our context. Professor Eddie Obeng defines the new world as a world that can change faster than you can learn. As we engage with an ever-growing portion of this world, it becomes more difficult to satisfy all stakeholders whilst delivering value and benefits in a new and unfamiliar context.

Project professionals have moved beyond delivering incremental improvements to generating deep and lasting benefits meeting the challenge of a changing world. Yet at the same time we are being asked to deliver more with less – more value, more benefits, more stakeholders, extended life cycle and greater sustainability to be delivered in less time, less cost, and with fewer mistakes. The challenge of creating the new capabilities in an unknown environment is only matched by the need to become more inventive in delivering the solutions; generating improvements in the way projects and programmes are managed, risks are handled, subcontractors are overseen and increasingly diverse stakeholder groups contribute and participate. Ours is a world which demands what appears to be the impossible; *Advances in Project Management* aims to explore how the profession can think and act in this demanding new world.

We live in an increasingly unpredictable and complex environment replete with change, ambiguity and uncertainty. Consequently, there appears to be a greater need to be concerned with defining the new kind of project management required to survive, succeed and excel in this new environment.

The book thus offers insights and ideas about how the profession will rise to the challenges of the new world – climate change, technological advances, globalisation, social networks, public health, security and economic regeneration and growth. The challenges require fundamentally new ways of making sense and shaping a world we neither control, nor fully understand.

Success in the future would require better understanding of the context and deeper engagement with the business. It will also require new ways of developing professionals, making change work and guaranteeing value.

We increasingly talk about the new world and the new realities of the twenty-first century. The new world offers many new challenges that we seem to encounter on a more frequent basis: speed, uncertainty, ambiguity and complexity. Moreover, the new world is increasingly characterised by limited attention, growing collaboration and participation, new social media technologies and the expanding scope and influence of projects. The challenges combined with the new characteristics point to a much-needed departure from project management orthodoxy.

But that leads to many questions. Where do we go next? Indeed, how do we deliver successfully in novel and unstructured situations? How do we manage in uncontrolled environments? More crucially perhaps, how do we move from managing to leading? How do we involve a more involved world? From the point of view of developing leaders, what skills are essential for success in the new world? And finally, how do we find out?

Many of these questions are addressed through the series of chapters presented in this book. Other questions are identified and explored along the journey as we seek to identify, understand and share new insights and advances.

Advances in Project Management

The individual chapters have been selected to feature in the 'Advances in Project Management' column published in the *PM World Journal*. The main purpose of this column is to make the ideas and principles of the knowledge and skills required to manage projects more accessible. *Advances in Project Management* was introduced in order to improve understanding and project capability further up the organisation; amongst strategy and senior decision makers and amongst professional project and programme managers. Our ambition has been to provide project sponsors, project management leaders, practitioners, scholars and researchers with thought-provoking, cutting-edge information that combines conceptual insights with interdisciplinary rigour and practical relevance thus offering new insights and understanding of key areas and approaches.

In order to identify the potential authors, a wide range of books and resources have been consulted. Contributions were selected by the editor on the basis of their individual merit, usefulness and applicability. The chapters offered here will feature many leading practitioners, researchers and managers and highlight concepts, ideas and tools that will be of benefit to practising project managers.

To this end, the individual chapters aim to:

1. identify and focus on *key* aspects of project, programme and portfolio management;

2. offer practical case examples of how new applications have been tackled in a variety of industries;

3. provide access to appropriate new models in these areas, as they emerge from academic research.

In other words, the book aims to provide those people and organisations who are involved with the developments in project management with the kind of structured information that will inform their thinking, their practice and improve their decisions. Featured contributions have not been limited to a particular community, country or association to ensure that a wide variety of angles and perspectives are covered.

Geography and Scope

People come to project management from many directions bringing with them their own particular take. Over the years we have witnessed a number of distinct influences on the development of project management from various sectors, government bodies, professional associations and even from specific geographical regions. The publication is meant to be inclusive and offers a platform to ideas which will be of use to practitioners regardless of where they are based and whatever the geography of the projects that they are running.

Projects take place in organisations and feature people. Our approach therefore is to focus on what it takes to manage projects in these settings. The topics we cover will emphasise the skills, competencies, attitudes and knowledge that are needed for successful delivery in a wide range of environments and contexts. We will also endeavour not to get stuck in any particular silo, instead offering a wider and more inclusive context. Some of our experts come from other domains and bring organisational, psychological, sociological or other influences that they can share. The value of this publication therefore is in integrating the viewpoints and perspectives and offering improved insights and understanding as a result.

Project management is a dynamic and exciting discipline. Together we can embark on a journey of exploration in unchartered territories, trying to map some of our emerging knowledge and understanding. We encourage readers to engage with the range of topics, and would also encourage those who would like to share their insights and ideas with the wider community to get in touch with the editor. We look forward to continuing this discussion and extending the boundaries of project management.

Darren Dalcher
London, UK

1

Uncertainty
Managing Project Uncertainty

Darren Dalcher

Risk management is primarily concerned with what we can anticipate or see. It offers mechanisms and approaches for addressing chunks of the future that we can conceive. Increasingly, however, more organisations allocate additional contingency resources for other things that we do not know about. While risks can be viewed as the known unknowns, uncertainty is concerned with the unknown unknowns that are not susceptible to analysis and assessment. It is these unknown unknowns that challenge project managers and require new skills and understanding. This is where the handling and managing of project uncertainty becomes a key skill.

Decision makers (including project managers) are not comfortable in the presence of uncertainty. The impact of uncertainty often defers decisions and delays actions as managers attempt to figure out their options. Indeed, the presence of uncertainty has been shown by psychologists to reduce the effectiveness of decision makers in different areas.

Uncertainty has traditionally been associated with programmes and portfolios, but is increasingly invoked in discussions related to projects in modern contexts. It is yet to feature as a separate topic in the traditional bodies of knowledge, and consequently many organisations are seeking guidance and insights on this important topic.

The chapter by David Cleden explores some of the implications of uncertainty offering tools and approaches for making sense of and responding to uncertainty. It is derived from his recent book which is part of the Advances in Project Management series published by Gower.

Brian Greene pointed out that 'exploring the unknown requires tolerating uncertainty'. Nonetheless, it is still unusual to find extensive treatise of uncertainty. David Cleden makes an essential contribution to a very important conversation about the role of uncertainty in project work. David encourages the adoption of a more responsive and intelligent stance towards uncertainty in projects, thereby offering a positive attitude and a refreshed perspective for re-considering success in projects in the light of the new emerging understanding of opportunities and the role of uncertainty.

That Uncertain Feeling

David Cleden

Here's a fundamental truth that all project managers would do well to heed: all risks arise from uncertainty, but not all uncertainty can be captured as risks. This means that over-reliance on risk management can leave a project exposed to unexpected 'bolts from the blue' forcing the project manager to be reactive not proactive.

No forecast of future events can ever be perfect. Consequently risk management can only take us so far – we also need a strategy for managing uncertainty. Of course, dealing with uncertainty is fundamentally hard because we are trying to grapple with what we don't know. So to stand a chance of keeping uncertainty within manageable limits we need to understand its characteristics and learn to recognise its warning signs. Here are five guidelines which will help.

1. **Aim to *contain* uncertainty, not eliminate it.** You can't bring order to the universe and neither can you protect your project from every conceivable threat. Managers who try, labour under unworkable risk management regimes, constructing incomprehensible risk logs and impossibly costly mitigation plans. Amidst all the effort being poured into managing small, hypothetical risks, a project manager may be too busy to notice that the nuts and bolts of the project – where the real focus of attention should be – has stalled. Concentrate instead on detecting and reacting swiftly to early signs of problems. Whilst uncertainty can never be entirely eliminated, it can be contained, and that should be good enough. Ultimately, this is a far more effective use of resources.

   Visualise a project as existing in a continual state of dynamic tension (see Figure 1.1). The forces of uncertainty continually try to push the project off its planned path. If left unchecked, the problems may grow so severe that there is no possibility of recovering back to the original plan.

The project manager's role is to act swiftly to correct the deviations – setting actions to resolve issues, implementing contingency plans, or nipping problems in the bud. This isn't risk management (at least, not entirely). Some of these problems will have bubbled up from the vast, nebulous cloud of 'unknown unknowns'. The project manager's only real defence is mindfulness and agility – in other words, spotting things going wrong at the earliest possible stage and being both creative and effective in damping the problems down.

2.   **Failure to execute project management processes thoroughly is not the sole cause of uncertainty.** Some people think uncertainty is a symptom of a poorly managed project. They argue that if everything is done right and in sufficient detail, there shouldn't be *any* uncertainty. Not true. Recognising the existence of uncertainty is the first step to dealing with it effectively. Don't shut yourself off from that possibility – and don't trust your chosen management methodology to eliminate all uncertainty from your project. It won't.

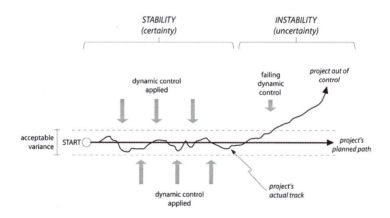

Figure 1.1   The illusion of project stability

Note: A dynamic balance exists between uncertainty and corrective actions which gives the illusion of stability.

3.   **Uncertainty is an attribute, not an entity in its own right.** Some project managers set aside a few hours each week to 'do' their risk analysis and mitigation planning. Then they get on with the 'real' job of managing the project. It's as if dealing with uncertainty is a separate work package, all neatly compartmentalised. That's a simplistic view. Uncertainty can lurk in each and every task, in their dependencies and underlying assumptions. Get into a frame of mind that is alert to the uncertainties in every aspect of the project. Then you'll be ready to deal swiftly with its consequences. An iterative planning approach is vital. Projects which are planned once (that is, at the beginning) and then expected to stick rigidly to that plan, rarely succeed. The project manager needs to be constantly alert for potential changes, tweaking the plan to keep control of events, not the other way round.

Of the many iterative management cycles in existence (the Shewhart cycle of Plan–Do–Check–Act being perhaps the most famous), my personal favourite is the OODA loop. It was developed by a US Air Force fighter pilot and sounds like something out of an episode of Dr Who. What's not to like?

OODA stands for Observe, Orient, Decide, Act. Like a pilot engaging in aerial combat, the project manager needs to judge the pace of events, assess opportunities and threats in the current situation and be on the lookout for warning signs of emerging problems. He or she must cycle through each of the four stages:

- Observe – gather information relevant to the problem; notice patterns and trends; be dispassionate and objective in gathering the facts.

- Orient – place the observations of the problem in context; understand which are the dominant factors; draw on previous (but relevant) experience; filter the relevant from the irrelevant.

- Decide – choose a course of action which will reduce the threat; evaluate a range of possibilities; consider undesirable side-effects as well as the benefits.

- Act – implement the decision swiftly and with precision.

Instead of being forced on the defensive and having to respond to unexpected events, rapid execution of the OODA loop allows the project manager to regain control over an uncertain situation – driving forward with a solution instead of merely reacting to events.

4.   **Effective decision making is at the heart of managing uncertainty.** When faced with uncertainty, the project manager has several options available (see Figure 1.2). The project manager must decide how to act – either by suppressing uncertainty through plugging knowledge gaps, or adapting to it by drawing up mitigation plans, or detouring around it and finding an alternative path to the project goals. Whichever action is taken the quality of decision making determines a project's survival in the face of uncertainty, and is influenced by everything from individual experience, line management structures, to the establishment of a blame-free culture which encourages those put on the spot to act in the project's best interests with confidence. Remember the old saying: 'Decisions without actions are pointless. Actions without decisions are reckless.'

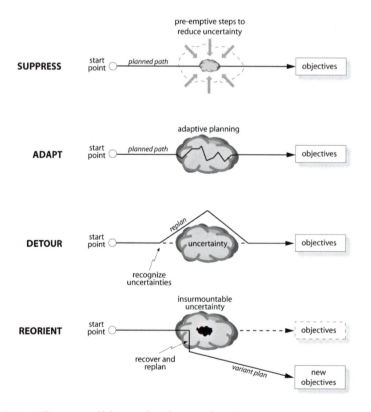

Figure 1.2   Four possible modes for confronting uncertainty

5.   **Uncertainty encompasses both opportunity and threat.** It's important to seize opportunities when they arise. If some aspects of your project are uncertain, it means there are still choices to be made – so choose well. All too often we only think of the negative consequences. Perhaps we can achieve *more* than was planned? Is there a chance to be innovative? Be open to creative solutions. As Einstein said, 'We can't solve problems by using the same kind of thinking we used when we created them.'

All approaches to dealing with uncertainty depend to a greater or lesser extent on being able to forecast future events. The classic approach is linear: extrapolating from one logical situation to the next, extending out to some point in the future. But with each step, cumulative errors build up until we are no longer forecasting but merely enumerating the possibilities.

Suppose instead we don't try to forecast what *will* happen, but focus on what we *want to happen*. This means visualising a desired outcome and examining which attributes of that scenario are most valuable. Working backwards from this point, it becomes possible to see what circumstances will naturally lead to this scenario. Take another step back, and we see what precursors need to be in place to lead to the penultimate step – and so on until we have stepped back far enough to be within touching distance of the current project status (see Figure 1.3).

This approach focuses on positive attributes – what are the project's success criteria – not the negative aspects of the risks to be avoided. Both are important, but many project managers forget to pay sufficient attention to nurturing the positive aspects. By 'thinking backwards' from a future scenario, the desired path often becomes much clearer. It's ironic to think that backwards is often just what's needed to lead a project forward to successful completion.

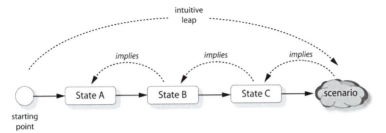

Figure 1.3   Making an intuitive leap to visualise a future scenario

Note: Thinking backwards identifies the key factors which need to combine to achieve the scenario. Understanding this sequence reveals where there are key uncertainties.

2

Strategic Risk
When do Projects Begin? Addressing Strategic Project Appraisal Issues

Darren Dalcher

There are different views embedded in the various books of knowledge about when a project actually begins. Depending on your point of view, the start date will be somewhere between the initial generation of the idea, the creation of the business case, the assignment of a project manager or even the initial project kick-off meeting. The view that you hold will in turn influence your processes, your constraints and your approaches to dealing with risks and uncertainties.

However, regardless of the actual start date, there are choices that need to be made about selecting the right projects, committing to the right portions and aspects of projects and maintaining portfolios and programmes which are balanced. These decisions are taken at an early stage under conditions of uncertainty and can be viewed as strategic decisions about the project. Such strategic decisions have a crucial influence on the success of projects and portfolios, and indeed on how success is perceived.

The project appraisal process and the decision-making behaviour that accompanies it clearly influence the resulting project. Once a project decision has been taken the remainder of the work tends to unfold downstream. Given the lack of involvement of project managers in strategic decision making it is perhaps not surprising that we fail to engage in the wider process and ignore the downstream impacts of these early decisions.

The work by Professor Elaine Harris focuses on the crucial area of strategic-level risks that organisations may face. The work develops a project typology identifying the seven major types of strategic-level projects and their typical characteristics. It provides a rare link between strategic-level appraisal and risk management by focusing on the common risks shared by each type. It thus guides practitioners to implement a strategy that is better suited to the context of their project thereby enabling the development of a more flexible and adaptable response in the uncertain real-world of project management.

The accompanying chapter is developed from the book *Strategic Project Risk Appraisal and Management* published by Gower in the Advances in Project Management (AiPM) series.

Michael Porter pointed out that 'the essence of strategy is choosing what not to do'. Maimonides asserted that the risk of the wrong decision is preferable to the terror of indecision. In drawing our attention to the issues of strategic project appraisal Professor Harris has done the community a great service offering a new approach to understanding and reasoning about issues related to specific types of projects and the strategies required to mitigate their impacts and improve our corporate ability to make the right decisions and initiate projects in the right way.

Strategic Project Risk Appraisal and Management

Elaine Harris

Strategic decisions to select which projects an organisation should invest in are taken without certain knowledge of what the future will hold and how successful the project will be. Faced with this uncertainty, we can only attempt to predict the factors that can impact on a project. Once we can identify these factors and their possible impacts we can call them 'risks' and attempt to analyse and respond to them. Risks can be both positive, such as embedded opportunities, perhaps to do more business with a new client or customer in future, or negative, things that can go wrong, and those indeed require more focus in most risk management processes. Project risk assessment should therefore begin well before the organisation makes its decision about whether to undertake a project, or if faced with several options, which alternative to choose.

One common weakness in the approach that organisations take to project risk management is the failure to identify the sources of project risk early enough, before the organisation commits resources to the project (appraisal stage). Another is not to share that risk assessment information with project managers so that they can develop suitable risk management strategies. Through action research in a large European logistics company, a new project risk assessment technique (*Pragmatix®*) has been developed to overcome these problems. It provides an alternative method for risk identification, ongoing risk management, project review and learning. This technique has been applied to seven of the most common types of projects that organisations experience (from business development, acquisitions and new product developments to IT, new site or relocation, compliance and events management). This chapter features three of these seven types to give a flavour of the research findings.

Knowledge of where the risks are likely to come from is usually developed intuitively by managers through their experience in the organisation and industry. Advanced methods used in the research reported here included repertory grid[1] and cognitive mapping[2] techniques to elicit this valuable knowledge. However common risks may be found in projects of a similar type, and up to half may be identified by applying common management techniques. These are explained for the three project types presented. The final section of this chapter shows the analysis of 100 risk management strategies into six categories, and draws conclusions for the use of a strategic approach to project risk identification, assessment and management.

Type 1 Business Development Projects (BDP)

These projects involve securing new customers and markets for existing products or services. The strategic analysis of the organisational and environmental context for a BDP can help to generate several possible risks. The analysis of strengths, weaknesses, opportunities and threats (SWOT) can identify risk areas for the organisation (corporate factors in Table 2.1), and help to analyse the strategic fit of the project. Then a more detailed analysis of the external factors, political, economic, social, technical, legal and environmental (PESTLE) can identify further risk areas (external and market factors in Table 2.1). The invitation to tender might also help to identify risks in a BDP project, for example the 'demands of the customer' in Table 2.1.

Type 2 Systems Development or IT Projects

For an IT project, which is essentially a supply problem, the chain from software supplier to client (users) via sponsor (owner) can reveal at least half of the sources of risk. The functional requirements of the system are defined by the client, and the risks here may determine whether the client will be satisfied that the system does what it is supposed to do. Internal clients in IT projects may be more demanding than external clients in BDP projects. Figure 2.1 shows a typical

---

1   Repertory grid technique (RGT) is a method of discovering how people subconsciously make sense of a complex topic from their range of experience. This was used to identify the project risk attributes in Table 2.1.

2   Cognitive mapping uses a visual representation of concepts around a central theme. This was used to display risk attributes in a project risk map in Figure 2.1.

project risk map for an IT project. The figure shows the high-risk areas shaded darker and the lower-risk areas lighter. The key to managing these risks is in understanding and responding to stakeholder motivations and expectations.

Table 2.1   Project risk attributes for business development projects

Project Risk Attributes	Brief Definition (see full glossary in appendix)
CORPORATE FACTORS: Strategic fit Expertise Impact	Potential contribution to strategy Level of expertise available compared to need Potential impact on company/brand reputation
PROJECT OPPORTUNITY: Size Complexity Planning timescale Quality of customer/supplier	Scale of investment, time and volume of work Number of and association between assumptions Time available to develop proposal pre-decision Credit checking and so on added during version 4 updates
EXTERNAL FACTORS: Cultural fit Quality of information Demands of customer(s) Environmental	Matching set of values, beliefs and practices of parties Reliability, validity and sufficiency of base data Challenge posed by specific customer requirements Likely impact of Political, Economic, Social, Technical (PEST factors), including Transfer of Undertakings (Protection of Employment (TUPE)
COMPETITIVE POSITION: Market strength Proposed contract terms	Power position of company in contract negotiations Likely contract terms and possible risk transference

Source: Adapted from Harris, E. (1999), Project Risk Assessment: A European Field Study. *British Accounting Review*, 31(3), pp. 347–71.

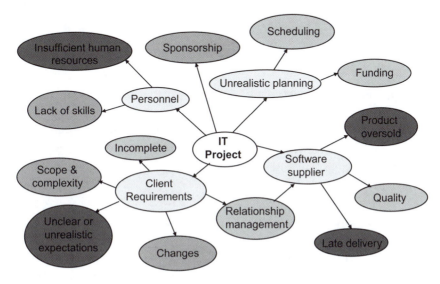

Figure 2.1   IT project risk map

Table 2.2   Mitigating actions

Source of Risk	Mitigating actions
Employees Loss of staff Loss of expertise Effect on morale Poor local labour market	Offer positive and consistent benefits package Negotiate key employees benefits package to encourage move Good communications with staff and transparency of business case Establish good market intelligence (before choice of location)
Management Leadership	Establish dedicated project management team with strong leader
Continuity Current projects	Maintain extra resources during move Flex project schedules for projects spanning relocation period
Organisational impact Culture Business procedures	Use relocation as a catalyst for change, improve existing culture Requires a development plan
Infrastructure Office equipment Capacity	Transport all office equipment from current site, reduce need for new Determine capacity required and ensure building completed in time

Source: Adapted from unpublished MBA group coursework with permission.

Type 3 New Site or Relocation Projects

A new site may involve the choice of location, acquisition, construction or refurbishment of buildings. In a relocation project, stakeholder analysis can reveal key groups of people who need managing closely. The employees are the principal group, followed by management and customers (continuity). Infrastructure risks (geographic factors) may be revealed by PESTLE analysis. Table 2.2 shows how risk management strategies can be developed to mitigate these risks.

Risk Management Strategies

For each type of project covered in the research a set of risk management strategies like those shown in Table 2.2 were identified. These totalled 100 and the following six categories emerged from their analysis, in the order of frequency of observation:

1. PROJECT MANAGEMENT (23%)

This category includes the deployment of project management methodologies such as work breakdown structure, scheduling, critical path analysis (CPA) and so on, and the establishment of a project leader and project team, as found in the project management body of knowledge. The most observations for this type of risk management strategy were in IT projects, and relocation and events management, where timing is critical.

2. HUMAN RESOURCE MANAGEMENT (21%)

This category includes recruitment, training and development of personnel, including managers and the management of change in work practices. This type of strategy featured most strongly in acquisitions, IT projects and relocation.

3. STAKEHOLDER MANAGEMENT (19%)

This category includes stakeholder analysis and management through consultation, relationship management and communications. It featured most strongly in systems development projects, new product development (NPD) projects and events management, which are necessarily customer-focused. In IT projects and events management there are many more stakeholder groups with diverse interests to manage.

4. KNOWLEDGE MANAGEMENT (18%)

This category includes searching for information, recording, analysing, sharing and documenting information, for example in market research and feasibility studies. It features most strongly in BDP and NPD projects and in acquisitions. It is closely related to training and development, so overlaps with that aspect of human resource management.

5. FINANCIAL MANAGEMENT (10%)

This category includes credit checking of suppliers and customers, financial modelling and budget management as well as business valuation, pricing strategies and contract terms. It is no surprise that it features most in business acquisitions, where a high level of financial expertise is required, and next in BDPs where terms are agreed and new customers vetted.

6. TRIALS AND PILOT TESTING (9%)

This category includes testing ideas at the feasibility study stage, testing possible solutions and new products. This could be clinical trials in pharmaceuticals, tasting panels with new food products or system testing in IT products, so features most strongly in IT and NPD projects.

Project reviews are recommended to evaluate how well risk management strategies have worked and to identify how risk management can be improved as part of organisational learning. The evaluation of *Pragmatix®* for risk identification, assessment and management revealed important benefits for the organisation, not least the opportunity to link risk assessment to later project management and post-audit review of projects. Such joined up thinking links strategic choice to strategy implementation through project management.

3

Risk
Risks or Projects?

Darren Dalcher

In an increasingly 'projectised' world should we be preoccupied with projects or with risks?

The management of risk has gradually emerged as a normal activity that is now a constituent part of many professions. The concept of risk has become so ubiquitous that we continually search for risk-based explanations of the world around us. German sociologist Ulrich Beck even noted that risk had become a dominant feature of society, replacing wealth production as a means of measuring decisions. Yet, at the same time progress is implemented through increments of projects; chunks of action that endeavour to bring about a new future that will improve and change our reality.

Progress is risky, especially when there is a lot at stake and thus risks and projects become closely intertwined. Projects can be introduced to mitigate risks or address perceived dangers, thereby becoming an instrument for dealing with known risks. Projects often have an element of uncertainty and can also be viewed as a way of creating new risks. Risk can provide a reason for embarking on a project, or become an output resulting from a project. Risk can also be shown to have a negative impact on a project therefore requiring a managed approach to control the impacts. Risk management can be utilised as a way of helping to manage or direct a project. Risk analysis can also be used as a systematic approach for improving decision making.

In summary, risk is integral to business and economic activity and to the pursuit of improvement, while projects provide a means of facilitating improvement and bringing about a new reality, which overcomes current risks and introduces new ones (both in terms of the explored new unknowns and the outcomes of the process of exploring). Risk is also concerned with enhancing potential benefits, while projects (and programmes) are evaluated in terms of the actual delivery of benefits.

However the management of risk is not a precise and well-defined science. It is an art that relies on attitudes, perceptions, expectations, preferences, influences, biases, stakeholders and perspectives: once again very much in common with the discipline of project management.

Managing risk is closely integrated with project management. Many standards now offer processes and methods for dealing with the risk portion of project management. Some of the techniques are well understood and well applied. Risk Registers in multiple colours are common in many projects, including failing projects. However, despite the awareness of risk and the recognition of the role of risk management in successfully delivering projects there is still evidence that risk is not being viewed as an integrated perspective that extends beyond processes.

The work of Dr David Hillson has been instrumental in forging a deeper understanding of the issues and perspectives of risk management in projects and in pushing the boundaries of what we know about risk and its management. David is firmly rooted in the practice of managing risk, but is constantly on the lookout for ways of extending the discipline and improving the art and practice of risk management.

The accompanying chapter by David Hillson is a fresh reflection on the current state of the knowledge and practice related to the management of risk. It provides a high-level summary of some the key issues. The work follows the publication of his book *Managing Risk in Projects* published by Gower in the 'Fundamentals of Project Management' book series.

The book concisely summarises available best practice whilst also introducing the latest advances in the discipline. This chapter highlights the improvements needed, grouping them into the core areas of principles, people, process and persistence.

By linking and integrating the key concepts in risk management and relating them to emerging trends such as Enterprise Risk Management (ERM), Dr Hillson has provided a coherent glimpse of the bigger picture reflecting the current state of the practice. New insights continuously stretching the boundaries of knowledge, such as the concept of risk energetics, skilfully combine with distilled and pragmatic pictures of the essential steps, actions, attitudes, behaviours and competences to refresh and re-energise the discipline. Above all Dr Hillson succeeds in showing us how to uphold the delicate balance between projects and risks in order to maintain our focus on progress and the successful delivery of benefits.

Managing Risk in Projects: What's New?

David Hillson

Humans have been undertaking projects for millennia, with more or less formality, and with greater or lesser degrees of success. We have also recognised the existence of risk for about the same period of time, understanding that things don't always go according to plan for a range of reasons. In relatively recent times these two phenomena have coalesced into the formal discipline called project risk management, offering a structured framework for identifying and managing risk within the context of projects. Given the prevalence and importance of the subject, we might expect that project risk management would be fully mature by now, only needing occasional minor tweaks and modifications to enhance its efficiency and performance. Surely there is nothing new to be said about managing risk in projects?

While it is true that there is wide consensus on project risk management basics, the continued failure of projects to deliver consistent benefits suggests that the problem of risk in projects has not been completely solved. Clearly there must be some mismatch between project risk management theory and practice, or perhaps there are new aspects to be discovered and implemented, otherwise all project risks would be managed effectively and most projects would succeed.

So what could possibly remain to be discovered about this venerable topic? Here are some suggestions for how we might do things differently and better, under four headings:

1.   Principles,

2.   Process,

3.   People,

4.   Persistence.

Problems with Principles

There are two potential shortfalls in the way most project teams understand the concept of risk. It is common for the scope of project risk management processes to be focused on managing possible future events which might pose threats to project cost and schedule. While these are undoubtedly important, they are by no means the full story. The broad proto-definition of risk as 'uncertainty that matters' encompasses the idea that some risks might be positive, with potential upside impacts, mattering because they could enhance performance, save time or money, or increase value. And risks to objectives other than cost and schedule are also important and must be managed proactively. This leads to the use of an integrated project risk process to manage both threats and opportunities alongside each other. This is more than a theoretical nicety: it maximises a project's chances of success by intentionally seeking out potential upsides and capturing as many as possible, as well as finding and avoiding downsides.

Another conceptual limitation which is common in the understanding of project risk is to think only about detailed events or conditions within the project when considering risk. This ignores the fact that the project itself poses a risk to the organisation at a higher level, perhaps within a programme or portfolio, or perhaps in terms of delivering strategic value. The distinction between 'overall project risk' and 'individual project risks' is important, leading to a recognition that risk exists at various levels reflecting the context of the project. It is therefore necessary to manage overall project risk (risk of the project) as well as addressing individual risk events and conditions (risks in the project). This higher-level connection is often missing in the way project risk management is understood or implemented, limiting the value that the project risk process can deliver. Setting project risk management in the context of an integrated Enterprise Risk Management (ERM) approach can remedy this lack.

Problems with Process

The project risk process as implemented by many organisations is often flawed in a couple of important respects. The most significant of these is a failure to turn analysis into action, with Risk Registers and risk reports being produced and filed, but with these having little or no effect on how the project is actually undertaken. The absence of a formal process step to 'Implement Risk Responses' reinforces this failing. It is also important to make a clear link between the project plan and risk responses that have been agreed and authorised. Risk responses need to be treated in the same way as all other project tasks, with an agreed owner, a budget and timeline, included in the project plan, reported on and reviewed. If risk responses are seen as 'optional extras' they may not receive the degree of attention they deserve.

A second equally vital omission is the lack of a 'Post-project Review' step in most risk processes. This is linked to the wider malaise of failure to identify lessons to be learned at the end of each project, denying the organisation the chance to learn from its experience and improve performance on future projects. There are many risk-related lessons to be learned in each project, and the inclusion of a formal 'Post-project Risk Review' will help to capture these, either as part of a more generic project meeting or as a separate event. Such lessons include identifying which threats and opportunities arise frequently on typical projects, finding which risk responses work and which do not, and understanding the level of effort typically required to manage risk effectively.

Problems with People

It is common for project risk management to be viewed as a collection of tools and techniques supporting a structured system or a process, with a range of standard reports and outputs that feed into project meetings and reviews. This perspective often takes no account of the human aspects of managing risk. Risk is managed by people, not by machines, computers, robots, processes or techniques. As a result we need to recognise the influence of human psychology on the risk process, particularly in the way risk attitudes affect judgement and behaviour. There are many sources of bias, both outward and hidden, affecting individuals and groups, and these need to be understood and managed proactively where possible.

The use of approaches based on emotional literacy to address the human behavioural aspects of managing risk in projects is in its infancy. However some good progress has been made in this area, laying out the main principles and boundaries of the topic and developing practical methods for understanding and managing risk attitude. Without taking this into account, the project risk management process as typically implemented is fatally flawed, relying on judgements made by people who are subject to a wide range of unseen influences, and whose perceptions may be unreliable with unforeseeable consequences.

Problems with Persistence

Even where a project team has a correct concept of risk that includes opportunity and addresses the wider context, and if they ensure that risk responses are implemented effectively and risk-related lessons are learned at the end of their project, and if they take steps to address risk attitudes proactively – it is still possible for the risk process to fail! This is because the risk challenge is dynamic, constantly changing and developing throughout the project. As a result, project risk management must be an iterative process, requiring ongoing commitment and action from the project team. Without such persistence, project risk exposure will get out of control, the project risk process will become ineffective and the project will have increasing difficulty in reaching its goals.

Insights from the new approach of 'risk energetics' suggest that there are key points in the risk process where the energy dedicated by the project team to managing risk can decay or be dampened. A range of internal and external Critical Success Factors (CSFs) can be deployed to raise and maintain energy levels within the risk process, seeking to promote positive energy and counter energy losses. Internal CSFs within the control of the project include good risk process design, expert facilitation and the availability of the required risk resources. Equally important are external CSFs beyond the project, such as the availability of appropriate infrastructure, a supportive risk-aware organisational culture, and visible senior management support.

So perhaps there is still something new to be said about managing risk in projects. Despite our long history in attempting to foresee the future of our projects and address risk proactively, we might do better by extending our concept of risk, addressing weak spots in the risk process, dealing with risk attitudes of both individuals and groups, and taking steps to maintain energy levels for risk management throughout the project. These simple and practical steps offer achievable ways to enhance the effectiveness of project risk management, and might even help us to change the course of future history.

4

Governance

Facing Uncertainty:
Project Governance and Control

Darren Dalcher

The following chapter continues our emerging theme of exploring issues related to uncertainty, turbulence, ambiguity and risk. Given the greater residual uncertainty in the environment and the current economic climate, are the risks of abuse of power, misinterpretation of issues, or inability to follow through on our intentions escalating beyond control? Indeed, can we ever hope to regain control over our project environment? At a more fundamental level is it really about control?

Large corporate failures in the last decade have raised awareness of the need for organisational governance functions to oversee the effectiveness and integrity of decision making in organisations. Technologists jest that you can control technology, but can at best only hope to manage people. Yet, people inhabit our corporations and execute their projects, and it is their interpretations of policies and their decisions that can jeopardise the achievement of organisational strategic targets and the successful delivery of projects. The key aim of governance therefore is to provide the visible framework for determining and guiding behaviour and decision making in order to support effective operation and delivery.

Governance spans the entire scope of corporate activity extending from strategic aspects and their ethical implications to the execution of projects and tasks. It provides the mechanisms, frameworks and reference points for self-regulation thereby delivering a quasi-replacement for the technologists' wish of explicit control.

In common with other governance arrangements, project and programme governance requires capability to interpret requirements and objectives, means and methods to deliver results, and procedures for monitoring and evaluating the achievement of the objectives. Indeed, the OECD (Organisation for Economic Co-operation and Development) refers to the set of relationships, structure and means which form a part of governance. In the context of managing projects, these extend beyond the needs and arrangements of an individual project.

Project governance is rapidly becoming a major area of interest for many organisations and practitioners, especially as poor governance is increasingly associated with the causes of project failure. The work of Dr Ralf Müller has sought to extend the body of knowledge and practice related to issues of governance. The perspective adopted in his work integrates the value system, responsibilities, processes and policies to provide wider visibility of impacts and issues related to the interests of both internal and external stakeholders, as well as the corporation itself. It thus provides a deeper understanding of the issues, relationships and mechanisms embedded in effective governance.

The chapter that follows was developed from the book *Project Governance* written by Dr Müller and published by Gower in the Fundamentals of Project Management series. The book embraces different governance styles and approaches whilst providing clear links between strategy and projects.

Dr Müller develops an integrated governance model addressing projects and project management as well as portfolios and programmes. In offering such a rich treatise of issues and topics related to governance he has advanced the discussion about the role of project governance. While we may still be unable to eliminate all failures and control our project environment, we can begin to use the tools and ideas offered in the work to mitigate against the impacts of change, turbulence, uncertainty (and people).

Project Governance
Ralf Müller

Governance starts at the corporate level and provides a framework to guide managers in their daily work of decision making and action taking. At the level of projects governance is often implemented through defined policies, processes, roles and responsibilities, which set the framework for peoples' behaviour, which, in turn, influences the project. Governance sets the boundaries for project management action by;

- **Defining the objectives of a project.** These should be derived from the organisation's strategy and clearly outline the specific contribution a project makes to the achievement of the strategic objectives.

- **Providing the means to achieve those objectives.** This is the provision of or enabling the access to the resources required by the project manager.

- **Controlling progress.** This is the evaluation of the appropriate use of resources, processes, tools, techniques and quality standards in the project.

Without a governance structure, an organisation runs the risk of conflicts and inconsistencies between the various means of achieving organisational goals, such as processes and resources, thereby causing costly inefficiencies that negatively impact both smooth running and bottom line profitability.

Approaches to governance vary by the particularities of organisations. Some organisations are more shareholder oriented than others, thus aim mainly for Return on Investment for their shareholder (that is, having shareholder orientation), while others try to balance a wider set of objectives, including societal goals or recognition as preferred employer (that is, having a stakeholder orientation). Within this continuum, the work in organisations might be controlled through compliance with existing processes and procedures (that is, behaviour control), or by ensuring that work outcomes meet expectations (that is, outcome orientation). Four governance paradigms derive from that and are shown in Figure 4.1.

The 'Conformist' paradigm emphasises compliance with existing work procedures to keep costs low. It is appropriate when the link between specific behaviour and project outcome is well known. The 'Flexible Economist' paradigm is more outcomes-focused, requiring a careful selection of project management methodologies and so on in order to ensure economic project delivery. Project managers in this paradigm must be skilled, experienced and flexible and often work autonomously to optimise shareholder returns through professional management of their projects. The 'Versatile Artist' paradigm maximises benefits by balancing the diverse set of requirements arising from a number of different stakeholders and their particular needs and desires. These project managers are also very skilled, experienced and work autonomously, but are expected to develop new or tailor existing methodologies, processes or tools to economically balance the diversity of requirements. Organisations using this governance paradigm possess a very heterogeneous set of projects in high technology or high-risk environments. The 'Agile Pragmatist' paradigm is found when maximisation of technical usability is needed, often through a time-phased approach to the development and product release of functionality over a period of time. Products developed in projects under this paradigm grow from a core functionality, which is developed first, to ever increasing features, which although of a lesser and lesser importance to the core functionality, enhance the product in flexibility, sophistication and ease-of-use. These projects often use Agile/ Scrum methods, with the sponsor prioritising deliverables by business value over a given timeframe.

Larger enterprises often apply different paradigms to different parts of their organisation (see Figure 4.1). Maintenance organisations are often governed using the Conformist or Economist paradigms, while R&D organisations often use the Versatile Artist or Agile Pragmatist approach to project governance.

	Shareholder Orientation	Stakeholder Orientation
Outcome Control	Flexible economist	Versatile artist
Behaviour Control	Conformist	Agile pragmatist

Figure 4.1   **Four project governance paradigms**

Governance is executed at all layers of the organisational hierarchy or in hierarchical relationships in organisational networks. It starts with the Board of Directors, which defines the objectives of the company and the role of projects in achieving these objectives. This implies decisions about the establishment of steering groups and Project Management Offices (PMOs) as additional governance institutions. The former often being responsible for the achievement of the project's business case through direct governance of the project, by setting goals, providing resources (mainly financial) and controlling progress. The latter (the PMOs) are set up in a variety of structures and mandates, in order to solve particular project-related issues within the organisation. Some PMOs focus on more tactical tasks, like ensuring compliance of project managers with existing methodologies and standards. That supports governance along the behaviour control paradigms. Other PMOs are more strategic in nature and perform stewardship roles in project portfolio management and foster project management within the organisation thereby supporting governance along the outcome control paradigms. A further governance task of the Board of Directors is the decision to adopt programme and/or portfolio management as a way to manage the many projects simultaneously going on in an organisation. Programme management is the governing body of the projects within its programme, and portfolio management the governing body of the groups of projects and programmes that make up the organisation. They select and prioritise the projects and programmes and with it their staffing.

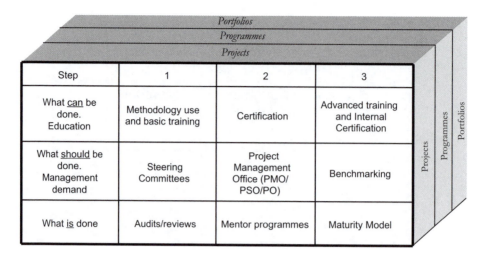

Figure 4.2   **Framework for governance of project, programme and portfolio management**

How Much Project Management is Enough for my Organisation?

This is addressed through governance of project management. Research showed that project-oriented companies balance investments and returns in project management through careful implementation of measures that address the three forces that make them successful. These forces are (see also Figure 4.2):

- educated project managers. This determines what *can* be done;

- higher management demanding professionalism in project management. This determines what *should* be done; and,

- control of project management execution. This shows what *is* done in an organisation in terms of project management.

Companies economise the investments in project management by using a three-step process to migrate from process orientation to project orientation. Depending on their particular needs they stop migration at step 1, 2 or 3 when they have found the balance between investments in project management (and improved project results) in relation to the percentage of their business that is based on projects. Organisations with only a small portion of their business based on projects should invest less, and project-based organisations invest more in order to gain higher returns from their investments. The three steps are (see also Figure 4.2):

Step 1: Basic training in project management, use of steering groups, and audits of troubled projects. This relatively small investment yields small returns and is appropriate for businesses with very little activities in projects.

Step 2: All of step 1 plus project manager certification, establishment of PMO and mentor programmes for project managers. This medium level of investment yields higher returns in terms of better project results and is appropriate for organisations with a reasonable amount of their business being dependent on projects.

Step 3: All of steps 1 and 2 plus advanced training and certification, benchmarking of project management capabilities, and use of project management maturity models. This highest level of investment yields the highest returns through better project results and is appropriate for project-based organisations, or organisations whose results are significantly determined by their projects.

The same concept applies for programme and portfolio management. This allows the tailoring of efforts for governance of project, programme and portfolio management to the needs of the organisation. By achieving a balance of return and investment through the establishment of the three elements of each step, organisations can become mindful of their project management needs. Organisations can stop at each step, after they have reached the appropriate amount of project management for their business.

How Does All That Link Together in an Organisation?

The project governance hierarchy from the Board of Directors, via portfolio and programme management, down to steering groups is linked with governance of project management through the project governance paradigm (see Figure 4.3).

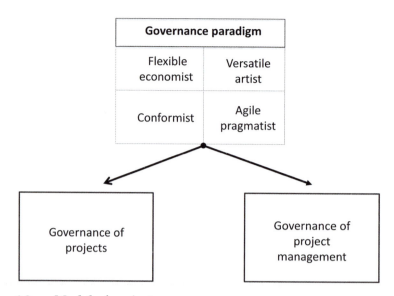

Figure 4.3   Model of project governance

A paradigm such as the Conformist paradigm supports project management approaches as described above in step 1 of the three-step governance model for project management, that is, methodology compliance, audits and steering group observation. A Versatile Artist paradigm, on the other hand, will foster autonomy and trust in the project manager, and align the organisation towards a 'project-way-of-working', where skilled and flexible project managers work autonomously on their projects.

The paradigm is set by management and the nature of the business the company is in. The project governance paradigm influences the extent to which an organisation implements steps 1 to 3 of the governance model for project management. It then synchronises these project management capabilities with the level of control and autonomy needed for projects throughout the organisation. This then becomes the tool for linking capabilities with requirements in accordance with the wider corporate governance approach.

5

Programme Management
Managing Uncertainty through Programmes

Darren Dalcher

How do we manage large-scale change efforts?

Uncertainty, ambiguity and risk in the project environment have featured throughout the previous chapters. The track record of successfully delivering projects has often been challenged. The earlier chapters suggest that there is still more to learn about how to manage risk and uncertainty. Yet, in seeking to implement long-term change with wider ranging implications, we inevitably face even higher levels of uncertainty and ambiguity.

Indeed, large change initiatives entail engagement at the organisational level. Leading and coordinating such change efforts introduces many new challenges. Focusing on the delivery of an outcome resulting from the vision and the associated benefits in a considerably longer time horizon requires a fundamental shift in how we reason about and prepare for large change initiatives.

Project-based structures are limited in their scope and their ability to deliver strategic benefits. They are also not useful in tackling the more complex and uncertain environments that are often encountered in modern business contexts. Moreover, they are not attuned to the growing need to focus on the business environment and the business itself.

The discipline of programme management can plug the gap as it provides the link between strategic decision making and the operational implementation of projects that deliver the vision of change. Programme management is therefore used to manage uncertainty and ambiguity, which are inherent in change, and to make the vision a reality. It also enables organisations to benefit from the emergent synergy that enables outcomes and benefits to deliver essential change resulting from the vision.

The interest in programme management continues to grow. In the last decade programme management has been documented in different sets of international standards emphasising various approaches, aspects and strengths of the discipline. New qualifications focused on the discipline are now available and there is a myriad of training courses on offer. The work of Dr Michel Thiry has been crucial to the development of programme management as a discipline and practice.

This chapter was developed from the book *Program Management* written by Dr Thiry and published by Gower in the Advances in Project Management book series.

The uncertainty and ambiguity inherent in turbulent organisational settings will continue to make project decisions more complex. Dr Thiry's approach offers new ways of dealing with uncertainty and ambiguity and delivering the vision of the organisation. The community is indebted to Dr Thiry for playing a key part in shaping the discipline over many years and for making sense of it in a concise and clear way. Dr Thiry resists the temptation to focus solely on processes. His work identifies the importance of behaviours, competence and culture and offers ways of promoting the culture shift within programme-based organisations. The combination of tools, guidance, insights and a roadmap to success delivers a new coordinated programme for tackling change, complexity and uncertainty and becoming more effective in realising sustainable benefits and delivering real value.

Programme Management beyond Standards and Guides

Michel Thiry

According to a number of recent chief executive officer (CEO) and chief information officer (CIO) surveys, strategic thinking has been at the top of the leadership agenda for executives, but implementing a strategy to realise value is not as obvious as it seems and optimising the use of resources to achieve this is even less evident. Can programme management provide executives with the means to achieve their objectives and increase the organisation's competitive edge? Can it provide sponsors with a clear method for defining outcomes and benefits and mastering their delivery? Can it provide users with an assurance that their needs will be fulfilled, as much as is possible, within stated parameters?

There are currently three main programme management guides, or standards, published by distinct professional bodies in America, Europe and Asia. In the UK and Japanese guides, programme management is associated with the management of complex organisational or societal change. The Project Management Institute (PMI) Standard associates programme management with the management of multiple projects within the context of a strategic plan, where benefits can be obtained from managing these projects together. Each of these publications describes roles, relationships with other processes, programme-specific processes, programme knowledge areas and other programme management components in more or less detail, but where does this leave the executive, sponsor and user?

Programme management has emerged as a distinct discipline in the late twentieth century. It progressively developed as project management was applied to more and more complex projects, to the management of strategic objectives or the management of multiple interrelated endeavours to produce strategic benefits. It is now generally agreed that programmes are a significant undertaking consisting of multiple actions spanning multiple business areas and that they are generally complex. Programme management deals in both high ambiguity and uncertainty and requires a high degree of organisational maturity.

Programme Maturity

Traditionally most organisations undertake projects as part of their work. Mostly these projects are treated as separate entities, independent from each other. They are often generated within a business unit and managed with that unit's resources. Larger projects undertaken either for external clients or for strategic purposes are usually managed on an ad hoc basis by a dedicated team. Programmes can either be 'vision-led', driven by strategic objectives, or 'emergent', a convenient grouping of existing projects for tactical reasons. Mature organisations will favour the more integrated vision-led approach that enables greater agility and responsiveness. Because of their overall strategic vision they are more likely to realise business benefits.

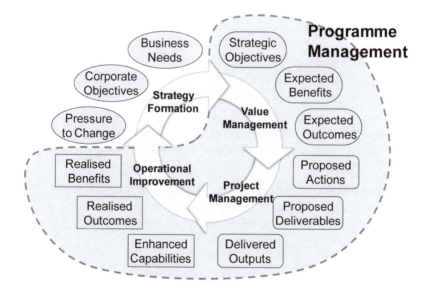

Figure 5.1   The mature programme integration

As programme management is used more and more to manage organisational change, the programme becomes a vehicle for interaction between business stakeholders to generate creative ideas and innovative products that increase the organisation's competitiveness. In order to be competitive, a mature organisation will use programmes to link a number of business processes and understand how to create synergy between its different components (see Figure 5.1). Traditional organisational structures are well adapted to stable well-defined environments; they are typically hierarchical and based on strong organisational control. In these structures, the portfolio is typically divided into sub-portfolios, programmes and projects. Recently, new organisational models have been developed that are more adapted to today's turbulent and fast-moving environment. These new organisational models are similar to a supply or value chain and the programme methodology is at the centre of the strategic decision management process.

In this type of organisation, programme management could be labelled as:

The governance and harmonised management of a number of projects and other actions to achieve stated business benefits and create value for the stakeholders.

But, developing a strong programme culture involves a shared understanding of a number of objectives and a strong framework that can be outlined in four key programme components: decision management, governance, stakeholder management and benefits management.

Key Programme Components

The main programme guides and standards already recognise governance, stakeholder and benefits management as key programme components. Decision management is a new area of development that requires both a learning cycle, the actual decision-making process and a performance cycle, the decision realisation process. Experienced managers know that successful change takes time and requires a sound decision-making process. They also understand that decision making is not just about tools, but about making the right choices, based on objectives that have been agreed and can be measured. Making sense of the issues at hand, generating ideas and elaborating them into viable options are essential elements of a sound decision-making process. Figure 5.2 depicts the whole programme decision management cycle.

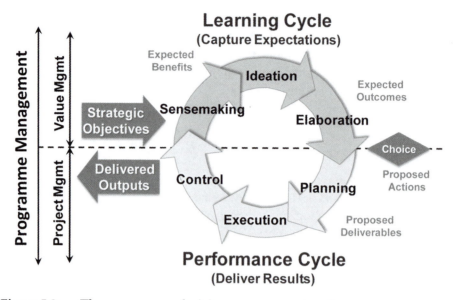

Figure 5.2   The programme decision management cycle

Mature organisations also adopt new developments and ideas for the other three programme components. Whereas most organisations focus on the control aspect of governance, mature organisations consider a broader area of governance that includes 'leading': defining the vision; 'structuring': providing the structures and resources necessary to achieve the vision; and 'conforming': making sure the vision and value are achieved. They adopt a stakeholders' management perspective that goes beyond roles and responsibilities of the different programme stakeholders to include the steps necessary to manage and engage stakeholders. Understanding the required contribution of the different programme stakeholders is an essential element of both programme governance and stakeholder management because both boundaries and relationships between the responsibilities of the different programme actors should be clearly identified to enable a smooth transition process between the strategy, the programme and operations.

Finally, benefits management includes the development of a sound benefits management system, from the definition of meaningful expected benefits to their actual measurable realisation. In order to ensure the realisation of strategic objectives, the programme life cycle is cyclical to enable regular assessment of benefits, evaluation of emergent opportunities and pacing of the process; it takes into account the 'interdependence' of component projects to ensure strategic alignment. To achieve this, a programme life cycle must be iterative, rather than linear, include periods of stability and have a learning and systems perspective. Executives and sponsors become change leaders by taking responsibility for three steps that underlie every programme decision: value creation, transition and value realisation.

Programme Management Life Cycle

Most books and guides on programme management have suggested programme 'phases' which are simply transpositions of the project perspective. This view can jeopardise the effectiveness of programme management and its capability to deliver strategies. Although it is now agreed that the objective of programmes is to produce business-level benefits by linking the strategy and projects, little management rhetoric has made its way into the programme management literature and practice.

The current view of the programme management life cycle can be summarised through five generic stages or processes:

1. The 'Formulation' stage, which consists of the definition of the programme's expected benefits through a stakeholder analysis and the agreement on the programme purpose and objectives, which can include a functional blueprint. This process is iterative.

2. The 'Organisation' stage, which consists of the development of the programme's detailed business case and technical blueprint as well as operational procedures and structures. This process is iterative with the formulation.

3. The 'Deployment' stage, which consists of the delivery of capabilities through the programme's constituent projects and other actions, including the transition into the business. This is a cyclical process.

4. The 'Appraisal' stage, which consists of a programme-level assessment of the benefits realisation and evaluation of the success of the transition to operational benefits. This is also a cyclical process.

5. Finally, the 'Dissolution' stage, which consists of the agreement on the timing and grounds for dissolution and implementation of the closing process, which includes long-term benefits measurement processes.

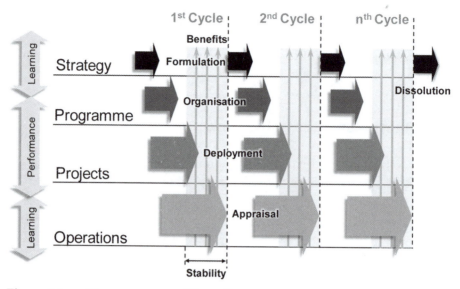

Figure 5.3   The programme life cycle

The formulation and the strategy development part of the organisation stage are learning cycles, as is the appraisal of benefits realisation. These stages require the application of value management tools and techniques. The structuring part of the organisation stage as well as the management of projects in the deployment stage, are performance cycles where project management tools and techniques can be appropriately used.

The programme life cycle diagram (Figure 5.3) exhibits the cyclical nature of programmes where benefits are appraised on a regular basis and the resulting operational outcomes are used to realign the strategy, if required. Typically the cycles of the programme life cycle also correspond to periods of stability that enable the organisation to absorb change at a rhythm that corresponds to its culture. These periods of stability, which usually correspond to stage gates, are typically determined when pacing the programme.

Conclusion

Whether you are an executive, a sponsor, a user, a programme or project manager, guides and standards can be useful, but it is your responsibility as a programme stakeholder to understand what your role in a programme is and how programme management can help your organisation achieve its objectives.

Programme management is the link between the business strategy and the value it will generate when implemented. It is the process through which executives will be able to express their needs and make sure they are fulfilled. Sponsors will be able to define the improvements they are expecting and clearly link them to the strategy to ensure they are realised and aligned with the business objectives. Programme managers will understand how to support both executives and sponsors in a tangible way and how to deliver measurable results to the business. Project managers will understand how their role is essential to the programme's success and finally, operational and technical users will be able to make sure the expected improvements are well integrated and produce the expected results.

6

Risk Leadership

Beyond Tame Problems: The Case for Risk Leadership

Darren Dalcher

Project management is often concerned with improving the current condition and can therefore be viewed in terms of a process moving from a problem, or an opportunity for improvement, towards a solution. In problem solving parlance it is assumed that we are seeking to transform from the current 'problem' space to some desired state which represents the ideal solution. If our problems are simple, the logic goes, so might the solutions be. In a carefully ordered world a sequence of steps could therefore guide us along a structured route from the perceived problem to the target solution.

Such simplistic problem configurations can be viewed as simple, well defined, tame or benign. The processes they require match that simplicity by implying a deterministic order of resolution, further suggesting a target state that is optimal, or at least the optimal means for achieving the desired solution. Tame problems thus benefit from a linear step-by-step resolution approaches.

In practice, many of the problems faced by project managers do not conform to idealised structures and optimal decision routines. Instead project managers have to deal with novel, one of a kind, unfocused and complex situations that are better characterised as ill structured. To reflect the open-ended, interconnected, social perspective we operate in, planners and designers talk of 'wicked problems'. Such problems tend to be ill-defined and rely upon much elusive political judgement for resolution.

Messier situations imply a much closer link between problem and solution. Interfering and interacting with non-tame situations leads to waves of repercussions, inducing new problems of greater severity elsewhere. Add multiple stakeholders with conflicting priorities, value systems and wishes, some fuzzy boundaries, multiple levels of complexity and inherent contradictions and it becomes easy to see why many resolution efforts go awry.

The idea of a rational or scientific approach is particularly effective under tame conditions. It becomes stretched when the level of complexity rises and less than rational humans with contradictions and conflicting perspectives need to be accounted for. Many scientific methods, however appealing, have a somewhat limited domain of operation, especially when stretched to account for the wicked and messier aspects of real life.

The chapter by Dr David Hancock continues our focus on uncertainty and risk. Many of the methods used in risk management oversimplify life assuming a degree of 'tameness' that is unrealistic. The embedded uncertainty and ignorance faced in many projects cannot be accounted for through overly simplistic risk management. As a consequence we apply the wrong kind of procedures to situations.

The ideas in the chapter are taken from Dr Hancock's book *Tame, Messy and Wicked Risk Leadership* published by Gower in the Advances in Project Management book series. Dr Hancock reminds us that quantitative assessment is limited in some domains thus making a powerful case for a new kind of risk leadership: a more inclusive approach that embraces uncertainty and unpredictability whilst seeking improvement through realisation of the different paths that may open up as we seek to improve our current condition.

The Application of the 'New Sciences' to Risk and Project Management

David Hancock

Introduction

There is a feeling amongst some risk practitioners, myself included, that theoretical risk management has strayed from our intuition of the world of project management. Historically, project risk management has developed from the numerical disciplines dominated by a preoccupation with statistics (insurance, accountancy, engineering and so on). This has led to a bias towards the numerical in the world of project management.

In the 1950s a new type of scientific management was emerging, that of project management. This consisted of the development of formal tools and techniques to help manage large complex projects that were considered uncertain or risky. It was dominated by the construction and engineering industries with companies such as Du Pont developing Critical Path Analysis (CPA) and RAND Corp developing Programme Evaluation and Review Technique (PERT) techniques. Following on the heels of these early project management techniques, institutions began to be formed in the 1970s as repositories for these developing methodologies. In 1969 the American Project Management Institute (PMI) was founded; in 2009 the organisation has more than 420,000 members, with 250 chapters in more than 171 countries. It was followed in 1975 by the UK Association of Project Managers (changed to Association for Project Management (APM) in 1999) with its own set of methodologies. In order to explicitly capture and codify the processes by which they believed projects should be managed, they developed qualifications and guidelines to support them. However, whilst the worlds of physics, mathematics, economics and science have moved on beyond Newtonian methods to a more behavioural understanding, the so-called 'new sciences', led by eminent scholars in the field such as Einstein, Lorenz and Feynman. Project and risk management appears largely to have remained stuck to the principles of the 1950s.

Risk Management

The general perception amongst most project and risk managers that we can somehow control the future is, in my opinion, one of the most ill-conceived in risk management. However, we have made at least two advances in the right direction. Firstly, we now have a better understanding about the likelihood of unpleasant surprises and, more importantly, we are learning how to recognise their occurrence early on and subsequently to manage the consequences when they do occur.

Qualitative and Quantitative Risk

The biggest problem facing us is how to measure all these risks in terms of their potential likelihood, their possible consequences, their correlation and the public's perception of them. Most organisations measure different risks using different tools. They use engineering estimates for property exposures, leading to MFLs (maximum foreseeable loss) and PMLs (probable maximum loss). Actuarial projections are employed for expected loss levels where sufficient loss data is available. Scenario analyses and Monte Carlo simulations are used when data is thin, especially to answer 'how much should I apply' questions. Probabilistic and quantitative risk assessments are used for toxicity estimates for drugs and chemicals, and to support public policy decisions. For political risks, managers rely on qualitative analyses of 'experts'. When it comes to financial risks (credit, currency, interest rate and market), we are inundated with Greek letters (betas, thetas and so on) and complex econometric models that are comprehensible only to the trained and initiated. The quantitative tools are often too abstract for laymen, whereas the qualitative tools lack mathematical rigour. Organisations need a combination of both tools, so that they can deliver sensible and practical assessments of their risks to their stakeholders. Finally it is important to remember that the result of quantitative risk assessment development should be continuously checked against one's own intuition about what constitutes reasonable qualitative behaviour. When such a check reveals disagreement, then the following possibilities must be considered:

- a mistake has been made in the formal mathematical development;

- the starting assumptions are incorrect and/or constitute too drastic oversimplification;

- one's own intuition about the field is inadequately developed;

- a penetrating new principle has been discovered.

Tame Messes and Wicked Problems

One of the first areas to be investigated is whether our current single classification of projects is a correct assumption. The general view at present appears to treat them as linear, deterministic predictable systems, where a complex system or problem can be reduced into simple forms for the purpose of analysis. It is then believed that the analysis of those individual parts will give an accurate insight into the working of the whole system – the strongly held feeling that science will explain everything. The use of Gantt charts with their critical paths and quantitative risk models with their corresponding risk correlations would support this view. However this type of problem which can be termed 'tame' appears to be the only part of the story when it comes to defining our projects.

Tame problems are problems which have straight-forward simple linear causal relationships and can be solved by analytical methods, sometimes called the cascade or waterfall method. Here lessons can be learnt from past events and behaviours and applied to future problems, so that best practices and procedures can be identified. In contrast 'messes' have high levels of system complexity and are clusters of interrelated or interdependent problems. Here the elements of the system are normally simple, where the complexity lies in the nature of the interaction of its elements. The principle characteristic of which is that they cannot be solved in isolation but need to be considered holistically. Here the solutions lie in the realm of systems thinking. Project management has introduced the concepts of programme and portfolio management to attempt to deal with this type of complexity and address the issues of interdependencies. Using strategies for dealing with messes is fine as long as most of us share an overriding social theory or social ethic; if we don't we face 'wickedness'. 'Wicked' problems are termed as 'divergent', as opposed to 'convergent' problems. Wicked problems are characterised by high levels of behavioural complexity. What confuses real decision making is that behavioural and dynamic complexities coexist and interact in what we call wicked messes. Dynamic complexity requires high-level conceptual and systems-thinking skills; behavioural complexity requires high levels of relationship and facilitative skills. The fact that problems cannot be solved in isolation from one another makes it even more difficult to deal with people's differing assumptions and values; people who think differently must learn about and create a common reality, one which none of them initially understands adequately. The main thrust to the resolution of these types of problems is stakeholder participation and 'satisficing'. Many risk planning and forecasting exercises are still being undertaken on the basis of tame problems that assume the variables on which they are based are few, that they are fully understood and able to be controlled. However uncertainties in the economy, politics and society have become so great as to render counterproductive, if not futile, this kind of risk management that many projects and organisations still practise.

Chaos and Projects

At best I believe projects should be considered as deterministic chaotic systems rather than tame problems. Here I am not using the term 'chaos' as defined in the English language which tends to be associated with absolute randomness and anarchy (Oxford English Dictionary describes chaos as 'complete disorder and confusion') but based on the 'chaos theory' developed in the 1960s. This theory showed that, in systems which have a degree of feedback incorporated in them, that tiny differences in input could produce overwhelming differences in output (the so-called 'butterfly effect'). Here chaos is defined as aperiodic (never repeating twice) banded dynamics (a finite range) of a deterministic system (definite rules) that is sensitive on initial conditions. This appears to describe projects much better than the linear deterministic and predictable view as both randomness and order could exist simultaneously within those systems. The characteristics of these types of problem are that they are not held in equilibrium either amongst its parts or with its environment, but are far from being held in equilibrium and the system operates 'at the edge of chaos' where small changes in input can cause the project to either settle into a pattern or just as easily veer into total discord. For those who are sceptical, consider the failing project that receives new leadership – it can just as easily move into abject failure as settle into successful delivery and at the outset we cannot predict with any certainty which one will prevail. At worst they are wicked messes.

Conclusion

How should the project and risk professional exist in this world of future uncertainly? Not by returning to a reliance on quantitative assessments and statistics where none exists. We need to embrace its complexities and understand the type of problem we face before deploying our armoury of tools and techniques to uncover a solution, be they the application of quantitative data or qualitative estimates. To address risk in the future tense we need to develop the concept of 'risk leadership' which consists of:

- guiding rather than prescribing;

- adapting rather than formalising;

- learning to live with complexity rather than simplifying;

- inclusion rather than exclusion;

- leading rather than managing.

The implications of the new concept of risk leadership are described in Table 6.1 (over the page).

What does this all mean? At the least it means we must apply a new approach for project and risk management for problems which are not tame. That we should look to enhance our understanding of the behavioural aspects of the profession and move away from a blind application of process and generic standards towards an informed implementation of guidance. That project and risk management is more of an art than a science and that this truly is the best time to be alive and be involved in project and risk management.

Table 6.1   The new concept of risk leadership

Risk Management	Risk Leadership
Works to a defined scope, budget, quality and programme.	Recognises the possibility of different outcomes and tries to ensure that risk activities are directed towards making an acceptable set of outcomes more likely.
Uses the instrumental life cycle image of risk management as a linear sequence of tasks to be performed on an objective entity using codified knowledge, procedures and techniques, and based on an image of projects as apolitical production processes.	Uses concepts and images which focus on social interaction among people, understanding the flux of events and human interaction, and the framing of projects within an array of social agenda, practices, stakeholder relations, politics and power.
Manages process to ensure complicated projects of people and technology are kept running smoothly.	Develops behaviours and confidence in team through scenario planning and team building to identify and respond to risks and opportunities.
Establishes detailed steps, processes and timetables for risk management.	Understands the 'many acceptable futures' proposition and manages risk to produce the changes needed to achieve the acceptable outcomes.
Practitioners as implementers of the risk process. Training and development which produces practitioners who can follow detailed procedures and techniques, prescribed by project management methods and tools.	Practitioners as reflective listeners. Learning and development facilitates the development of reflective practitioners who can learn, operate and adapt effectively in complex project environments, through experience, intuition and the pragmatic application of theory in practice.
Applies concepts and methodologies which focus on risk management for product creation or improvement of a physical product, system or facility and so on, and monitored and controlled against specification (quality), cost and time.	Applies concepts and frameworks which focus on risk management as value creation. Whilst, aware that 'value' and 'benefit' will have multiple meanings linked to different purposes for the organisation, project and individual.
Attempts to control risk by monitoring results, identifying deviations from the plan and developing mitigation actions to return to plan.	Adapts the risk process to overcome major political, bureaucratic and resource barriers to develop change in behaviours through trust and managing expectations.
Based on the assumption that the risk model is (assumed to be) the actual 'terrain' (that is, the actual reality 'out there' in the world).	Based on the development of new risk models and theories which recognise and take cognisance of the complexity of projects and project management, at all levels and that the model is only part of the complex 'terrain'.
Seeks predictability and order.	Has learnt to live with chaos, complexity and uncertainty and leads through example to a successful conclusion.

7

Leadership
In Search of Project Leadership

Darren Dalcher

What makes a good leader? Indeed, are leaders born or made?

Leadership is often shrouded in mystery. It has a lot to do with facing dilemmas and overcoming challenges. Leaders search for opportunities and rewards that can reflect the intentions and desires of their organisations, thereby offering the inspiration to others to follow and deliver.

Many cultures and disciplines have struggled to define leadership. Many have also searched for the ideal way to develop, or grow, leaders. Leadership requires power to influence and realise, especially under difficult conditions. Consequently, leadership often boils down to dealing with and thriving under conditions of change.

Our previous chapter made a case for a new kind of project risk leadership: a more inclusive approach that embraces uncertainty and unpredictability in the search for a better future. A similar case can be made for skilled project leadership. Yet, while the concept of project management is well understood, there is very little guidance on project leadership and even less understanding of what it takes to develop good project leaders.

The development of leaders can be focused through attention to traits, skills, capabilities and competences that characterise good leaders. However, a different mix of skills will be required to deal with specific situations taking into account the characteristics of the specific sector.

The chapter by Dr Ralf Müller and Professor Rodney Turner draws on their book *Project-oriented Leadership* published by Gower in the Advances in Project Management book series. The book emphasises the key areas of managerial, intellectual and emotional competence leadership explaining how they can be integrated to form a deeper understanding of leaders and leadership.

The authors have given the discipline a model for the development of leadership competence-based theory of project performance. The model shows the process required for development, highlighting the enablers and obstacles involved in each step. The authors have also succeeded in enriching the literature in this area and through the integration of findings from a range of diverse areas have also provided a new perspective of project leadership.

Harold S. Geneen mused that 'leadership is practiced not so much in words as in attitude and in actions'. What makes a good project leader depends on the specifics of a given situation and what needs to be achieved in the context of the project and the environment. Until we discover how to give birth to excellent project leaders, we can begin to explore the attitudes, perspectives and competences needed to deliver project successfully.

Project-oriented Leadership

Ralf Müller and Rodney Turner

Leadership in projects provides guidance in direction, gives purpose and meaning to the work in the project. Management in projects makes sure that plans are developed, implementation is controlled and goals are accomplished. Both leadership and management are needed for long-term success. Leadership lights-up the flame of motivation, whereas management provides the oxygen for the flame to stay alive.

A lot has been written about project management, but relatively little can be found on leadership in projects. However, all organisations, including projects, need leaders who give vision and identity, keep the stakeholders and the project team on board and make difficult decisions. Leadership by the project manager is the often overseen success factor on projects

When viewed as a competence, then leadership can be learned, practised and continuously improved. Competence is hereby understood as the knowledge, skills, personal characteristics, traits and behaviours that deliver superior results. What is required for leadership competence in project management are intellectual (IQ), emotional, (EQ) and managerial (MQ) competences. These are made up of 15 underlying measurement dimensions, as shown in Table 7.1 (after Dulewicz and Higgs 2003).

The IQ address the cognitive and rational leadership aspects and the EQ the interpersonal and social aspects of leadership. The MQ supplement the other two competences to balance leadership and management at a level that is required for a project.

Through a PMI-funded worldwide study we identified the different combinations of specific leadership competencies of project managers which relate to success in different types of projects. These are shown in Table 7.2.

Table 7.1   Competences and their measurement

Competence	Measurement
Intellectual (IQ)	Critical analysis and judgement Vision and imagination Strategic perspective
Managerial (MQ)	Engaging communication Managing resources Empowering Developing Achieving
Emotional (EQ)	Self-awareness Emotional resilience Motivation Interpersonal sensitivity Influence Intuitiveness Conscientiousness

Table 7.2   Hierarchy of importance of specific leadership competencies by project type

	Project Type		
	Engineering and Construction Projects	Information and Telecommunication Projects	Organisational Change and Business Projects
Main competencies	Conscientiousness Sensitivity (vision)	Communication Self-awareness Developing others (vision)	Communication Motivation (vision)
Situational competencies	Managing resources, empowering, critical analysis and judgement, strategic perspective, emotional resilience, influence, conscientiousness		
Supporting competencies	Achieving, intuitiveness		

Each project type has key competencies which directly relate to project success, no matter what the particularities of the project are, such as contract type, complexity, life cycle phase or culture the project is in. For example, success in engineering and construction projects is largely influenced by the conscientiousness and sensitivity of the project manager. Project managers' visionary competencies are not asked for in these projects. Here the vision may be better given by the project sponsor. Communication competencies are needed for information and telecommunication projects as well as for organisational and business projects. Success in the former type of projects is also strongly influenced by the self-awareness of the project manager and his or her ability to develop project team members. The latter type of projects requires motivational, in addition to communication competencies.

Situational competencies come to bear through the particularities of projects in a given project type. Examples include: influence competencies are needed in highly complex organisational change projects, or critical analysis and judgement is needed in engineering and construction projects for renewal of existing products.

Supporting competencies work in collaboration with other competencies, but do not emerge as directly linked with project success.

Once project managers are aware of the specific leadership competencies needed for their projects, they can start learning to become a competent leader. Over time they are able to adjust their leadership styles not only to project types, but also to, for example, different cultures.

A process of unlearning old behaviour and learning of new behaviour is required for this. In other words, a development from becoming aware of different leadership competencies, via developing them for different types of projects and finally securing project success through the right combination and application of them.

In summary, project managers and their leadership style are a critical success factor in projects, which complements the well-known project management tools and techniques, or processes and methodologies.

Further Reading

Dulewicz, V. and Higgs, M. (2003). 'Leadership at the Top: The Need for Emotional Intelligence in Organizations.' *International Journal of Organizational Analysis* 11(3):194–210.

8

Earned Value

Progress and Performance: The Case for Extending Earned Value Management

Darren Dalcher

Are we there yet?

The dreaded question … Having returned from a family summer holiday I was reminded that regardless of their age, children sitting in a car (and therefore in a bounded environment) appear to be uniquely focused on progress and destination. Many parents will attest that the obsession with the target ensures that the continuous progress checking begins almost at the point of departure and that complications and delays are rapidly brushed aside to ensure the targeted focus remains firmly fixed. This offers an example of a classical control loop which monitors a key parameter by constantly questioning its value.

According to the Oxford Dictionary, progress is the forward or onward movement towards a destination, which also can represent advancement or development towards completion or improvement. Once a project is launched, a large part of the project manager's role is to gather information about the status of the project, interpret that information and take appropriate action. Milestones, progress reports and meetings play a part in providing visibility regarding progress. Techniques such as Earned Value Management (EVM) are used to inform management decisions on a project by delivering measures that can be used to assess its performance.

The UK's Association for Project Management, *APM Body of Knowledge*, Fifth Edition asserts that 'Earned Value Management is a project control process based on a structured approach to planning, cost collection and performance measurement' which facilitates the integration of project scope, time and cost objectives and the establishment of a baseline plan for performance measurement.

Traditional scheduling and budgeting inform management of the amount of budget that has been spent and the progress that has been achieved. EVM in contrast is concerned with determining the value of work achieved alongside the cost of achieving it, thereby providing a performance measure explaining what has been achieved as a result of the expenditure to date. It works by establishing baseline plans which can be compared with actual achievement during the execution of the project. Establishing a relationship between cost and achievement becomes the basis for monitoring and controlling progress, determining performance levels, identifying deviations from the agreed plans, predicting the ultimate outcomes of a project and making informed decisions about actions required to ensure the achievement of the project targets.

EVM has been in use since the 1960s; however it is normally viewed as an extension of cost measurement and project cost accounting. Other approaches have tried looking at the measurement of time, time performance and Earned Schedule. Such attempts also manage to change the meaning of some of the basic concepts in EVM. The chapter by Dr Alexandre Rodrigues attempts to open up a new perspective and introduce an alternative approach and an extended model.

Dr Rodrigues has been intimately involved in researching and extending the use of EVM and has been influential in shaping the discipline of performance measurement through the use of the EVM technique.

Progress can also represent the development of an area or discipline over time. The project management discipline is indebted to Dr Rodrigues and his colleagues for continuing to challenge the boundaries of the discipline. Work in this area is concerned with addressing concerns observed in practice and the new ideas presented by Dr Rodrigues have been applied successfully in empirical settings playing a key part in solving problems and improving our ability to measure performance and improve the track record of project delivery.

Earned value enhances good project management through the development of an integrated baseline planning, monitoring and control technique as well as the delivery of insights which underpin decision making. It is a technique that will continue to evolve and improve. Reflecting on our journey, we may not be there yet, but we now know that the journey looks to be interesting and challenging. Some of the solutions on offer are bound to generate more discussion and stimulate additional debates. It is hoped that through articles and publications, we can all play a part in this discussion and discover for ourselves new and improved ways for monitoring and controlling our projects. We actively seek and encourage further discussion and engagement. Until we get there, we simply must learn to enjoy the journey.

Effective Measurement of Time Performance using Earned Value Management

A Proposed Modified Version for Schedule Performance Index Tested Across Various Industries and Project Types

Alexandre Rodrigues

Earned Value Management (EVM) is a project performance measurement technique, sometimes referred to as being primarily oriented towards cost management but with limited applicability to managing time performance. There have been various arguments supporting this perspective, namely: it ignores the detailed aspects of the schedule like floats and the critical path, its indicators are based on currency value hence not intuitive for time management, and finally the time performance indicator Schedule Performance Index (SPI, given by EV over PV) always gives the value of 1 (that is, a project 'on time') in late or early finishes. The last argument in particular is typically used to declare SPI as an invalid or unreliable time performance indicator. However, all of these arguments are only apparent. As we will demonstrate in this chapter EVM can provide useful and valid time performance measures. The problem with the SPI indicator floating towards the value of 1 has been the subject of alternative approaches, for example its calculation based on the concept of Earned Schedule.

While this alternative approach resolves the problem of SPI floating towards one in late or early finishes, the secondary effect is that it also gives this indicator a different meaning to the original concept. Based on academic research using computer simulation models, and on practical applications in real-life projects, the author has developed an extended version of the original SPI (based on volume of work), which ensures the validity of this indicator throughout the whole execution period for the project. The solution found to overcome the weakness of the original SPI indicator preserves the original meaning of the *time performance* concept, that is, how fast against the plan is the volume of work being accomplished. This extended modified version of SPI has been used in several projects across various industries, in different countries, and it has successfully delivered useful and valid performance information. The extended model developed includes additional formulae for various 'to complete on time' indicators (To Complete Schedule Performance Indicator – TSPI) and 'at completion' forecasts. This chapter briefly explains the modified version of SPI and it also discusses the overall validity of using EVM to effectively support project time management. Some practical examples are also presented to illustrate the concepts. The use of SPI-based time performance indicators for the purpose of risk management under conditions of uncertainty is also discussed.

Introduction

The EVM method, often mistaken as an advanced technique only applicable to large complex multimillion projects, is grounded on the following key principles:

1. The project plan must integrate scope, cost and time elements. The work defined in the work breakdown structure, which is budgeted, is also formally related to the project schedule. In simpler terms, the work budgeted is the same work that is scheduled. This formal relationship between the project scope cost and time elements allows for an accurate time distribution of the project budget, as illustrated in Figure 8.1.

2. As time elapses, account can be made for the *volume* of work that should have been accomplished to date. This *volume of work* is to be measured as *monetary value*. In simpler terms, $1 = 1 unit of work. In our example, the amount of work that should have been accomplished by month 5 is 650 *units of work* (that is, $650), which accounts for 65% of planned progress against the total scope of

1,000 *units of work* (that is, $1,000). The measure of the volume of work that should have been accomplished to date is referred to in EVM as 'Planned Value'. This is illustrated in Figure 8.2.

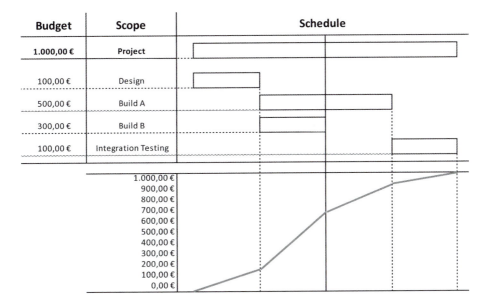

Figure 8.1   **The relationship between project scope, cost and time elements**

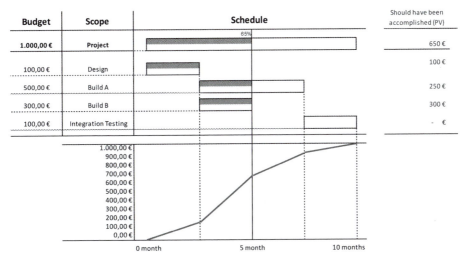

Figure 8.2   **Planned value**

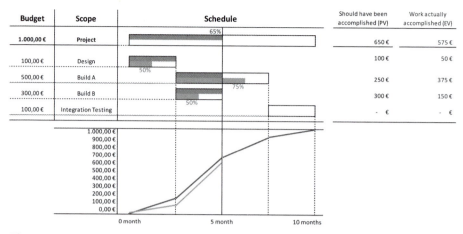

Figure 8.3   Earned value

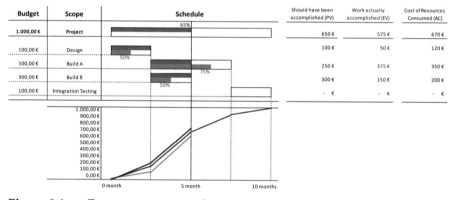

Figure 8.4   Resource consumption

3.   Work accomplishment must be measured in an objective and independent manner, leading to a % progress measure according to established criteria depending on the nature of the work – for example, % work progress = no. tests passed/no. of total tests. Measuring % progress allows for the accounting for the *volume of the work* actually accomplished to date, which is again measured in *monetary value*. The measure of the volume of work that was actually accomplished to date is referred to in EVM as Earned Value (EV). This is illustrated in Figure 8.3, where the total volume of the work actually accomplished to date equals 575 *units of work*, which accounts for 57.5% of the total scope.

4.   As work is accomplished, various types of resources (internal or external to the organisation) are consumed, accounting for the work and for the project actual cost incurred. Note that the cost incurred due to *resource consumption* is not necessarily the same as the official cost invoiced and/or paid in standard accounting terms. Sometimes resources are consumed for which payments or invoices have not yet been received; alternatively, invoices and payments might have been already issued for resources not yet consumed (for example, pre-payments). This is illustrated in Figure 8.4 where a total cost of $670 was incurred to accomplish to date $575 of volume of work.

In summary, the EVM method is based on the principle that, as the project progresses, the following three questions can be answered in measurable terms and in the form of monetary value:

a)   How much work should have been accomplished to date? (Planned Value – PV);

b)   How much work was actually accomplished to date? (EV);

c)   How much cost was incurred for the resources consumed to date? (Actual Cost – AC).

The requirements to answer these questions in measurable terms as monetary value are:

a)   the project plan formally integrates scope, cost and time elements;

b)   work accomplishment is measured independently in % progress;

c)   the cost of the resources consumed is accounted for and allocated to the project work.

In the author's experience, answering the three questions above and meeting these three requirements is a matter of adopting essential planning and control best practices, and these are applicable to projects of all sizes and of any nature (for example, from construction to software development).

Measuring Time Performance with Earned Value

Based on the three main measures described (that is, PV, EV and AC), it is possible to produce a variety of performance metrics in both cost and time dimensions.

Cost performance indicators have achieved wide acceptance, since the EVM method has always been primarily associated with cost control. In our example, it is apparent that:

a)   There is currently a cost overrun, since $670 were spent (AC) to produce only $575 of work (EV). Since $1 = 1 unit of work, then if 575 units of work were produced only $575 should have been spent. The excess cost consumed to date (Cost Variance – CV) can be accounted as CV = EV–AC = -$95.

b)   The reason why excess cost was consumed relates to cost efficiency being lower than expected. In fact, for each $1 spent, 1 unit of work should have been produced. If that has been the case, then 670 units of work would have been produced. However, only 575 units of work were produced, implying that each $1 spent produced less than 1 unit of work. In fact, for each $1 spent only 575/670 = 0.86 units of work were produced. Or in other words, each $1 consumed produced only $0.86 of work value. This ratio of EV/AC (that is, value of work produced/cost of resources consumed) is known as cost performance index (CPI) and it measures cost efficiency.

Besides CV and CPI, other cost metrics and indicators are available in the EVM method, all of which generally achieve wide acceptance.

With regard to time performance, similar indicators have been produced, in particular:

a)   Schedule Variance (SV) = EV – PV.
       If 575 units of work were produced while according to the project plan 650 units of work should have been produced, then less work was accomplished to date than planned and therefore overall there is work behind schedule that was not done and should have been done. In our example, this amounts to 75 units of work that should

have been accomplished but which have not yet been produced. In monetary terms, the project is behind schedule by -$75. That is, the budget of the *volume of work* behind schedule is $75.

b)   SPI = EV/PV.

If 575 units of work were accomplished against 650 units of work that should have been accomplished according to the plan, then only a *fraction* of the planned work has been accomplished, and this is 575/650 = 0.88. In other words, only 88% of the volume of work planned to be accomplished to date was actually produced. Another immediate conclusion is that the work was executed at a slower rate (or speed) than assumed in the plan. The work rate was in fact 88% of the planned work rate. The SPI indicator is the counterpart of the cost efficiency indicator CPI for time performance and it is aimed at measuring time efficiency.

Perhaps all would be fine with EVM for time management purposes if there would be no problems with these performance indicators. But the reality has shown that there are issues in particular with the SPI indicator.

The Problem with the Schedule Performance Index Indicator

The main problem with SPI is revealed when EVM is applied not just at the project level but also at the work package sub-level. At this level, work packages are often completed behind schedule or in advance of the scheduled completion date. On other occasions, the work is even started ahead of schedule. In these scenarios, the SPI indicator can produce values that seem to bear no relationship to reality. Some examples of these scenarios are given below.

THE LATE FINISH PROBLEM

When the baseline completion date is reached and the work is not totally completed, then execution extends beyond the baseline completion date and the SPI indicator continues to be calculated. However in this scenario, the SPI value will float towards 1 as the work reaches late completion, as illustrated in Figure 8.5 (see the uppermost curve), where the project is scheduled to be completed in ten months but it takes 12.6 months to actually complete the entire project work.

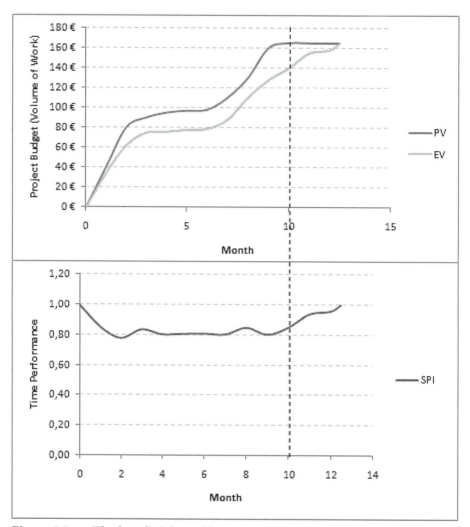

Figure 8.5   The late finish problem

The reason for this phenomenon is that as the work continues to be executed beyond the baseline completion date, the EV value (volume of work accomplished) continues to increase, whereas the PV value (planned volume of work) remains constant as it reached its maximum by the baseline completion date – that is, the whole work was planned to be completed by the baseline completion date.

The problem with this phenomenon is also obvious: the SPI indicator will produce performance values that will suggest an increasingly better time performance, well above the real performance. Consider for example the following scenario:

- project budget = $1,000:

  - baseline completion date = 5 months;

  - time now = 10 months;

  - PV (planned work) = $1,000 (that is, 1,000 units of work);

  - EV (actual work accomplished) = $950 (950 units of work);

  - SPI = 950/100 = 0.95 = 95%.

In this example, by reading the SPI indicator as previously described, one would conclude:

a)   by month 10, 95% of the work that was planned to be accomplished (1,000 units of work), was actually produced. While this is true, the 1,000 units of work were already planned to be accomplished much earlier, by month 5;

b)   the project work has been accomplished at a pace that is 95% of the planned work rate. This is, the actual work rate is 95% of the work rate assumed in the project plan. *This is an incorrect conclusion.*

Overall, a performance of 95% seems to be very close to the planned performance, whereas one can easily verify that the project will take *more than twice* its originally Planned Duration and therefore time performance is actually less than half (that is, <50%) of the planned performance. In the end of the project (or of the work package), the SPI will always be equal to 1, indicating a time performance of 100% even though the project was completed well beyond the baseline completion date.

This problem with SPI is aggravated when other time performance metrics are calculated based on SPI, such as the estimated final duration which is calculated as:

- Estimated Duration = Planned Duration/SPI (Time Efficiency).

In our example:

- Estimated Duration = 5 months/0.95 = 5.26 months.

Obviously, the project will never be completed in month 5.26, since we are already in month 10 and the whole work is not yet accomplished.

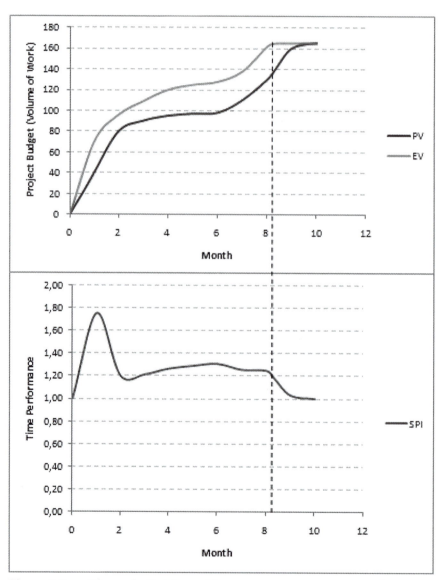

Figure 8.6   The early finish problem

THE EARLY FINISH PROBLEM

In a scenario of an early finish, time performance should be above 100%, or in other words the work was accomplished at a time rate (speed) higher than assume in the plan – the work was certainly done faster.

As illustrated in Figure 8.6, in the scenario of an early finish, at the time the work is completed before the baseline completion date, the SPI indicator will give a value above 1, as expected. However, as time continues to elapse in the project, the value of PV (planned work) will continue to evolve until it reaches the total project scope by the baseline completion date.

At this new moment in time, the SPI indicator will produce a value of 1, since EV = PV = total work (or baseline budget). In summary, from the period ranging from the actual completion date to the baseline completion date, the SPI indicator will float again towards the value of 1. While this would not be a problem for the whole project (since performance is no longer measured after the project is completed), it is certainly a problem for individual work packages, or project phases. But the problem is still a bit worse, since for the final project performance the final figure of SPI is not totally correct.

Let us consider again the following scenario:

- project budget = $1,000:

    - baseline completion date = 5 months;

    - time now = 4 months;

    - PV (planned work) = $700 (that is, 700 units of work);

    - EV (actual work accomplished)= $1,000 (100 units of work);

    - SPI = 1,000/700 = 1.43 = 143%.

In this situation a project that was planned to be completed in 5 months was actually accomplished in 4 months. By reading the SPI indicator, one would conclude:

a) by month 4, 143% of the work that was planned to be accomplished (700 units of work), was actually produced. This is a correct statement since 1,000 = 143% x 700 units of work;

b) the project work has been accomplished at a pace that is 143% of the planned work rate. This is the actual work rate is 143% of the work rate assumed in the plan. *This is an incorrect conclusion if applied to the final project performance.*

In fact, if the work had been accomplished at a 143% work rate, then each month on average would have produced 143% of the planned work and therefore the project would have been completed by month 3.5 (that is, 5 months/143% = 3.5 months), which is not the case. While it is true that by month 4, the work rate was 143% of the overall planned work rate for that moment in time, in terms of the total project, the whole scope was accomplished in four months instead of five months and this is not a 43% increase in time efficiency but rather it is a 25% increase, as it can be demonstrated:

- planned work rate = 1,000 units of work/5 months = 200 units of work/month;

- actual work rate = 1,000 units of work/4 months = 250 units of work/month;

- % actual work rate/planned work rate = 250/200 = 1.25 = 125%.

In conclusion, in an early finish scenario the final performance is incorrect and SPI will float towards 1 until the baseline completion date is reached.

WORK STARTED AHEAD OF SCHEDULE

When work is stated ahead of schedule, the EV will produce a value equal to the amount of work accomplished in a period of time where no work was supposed to have been done. Therefore, for that period, the PV will have a value of zero (no work supposed to be done). The results in terms of time performance will be:

- $SV = EV - PV = EV$.

It will produce a positive value indicating the amount of work that has been accomplished ahead of schedule.

- SPI = EV/PV = EV/0.

This is indeterminate, since no value can be produced. In a period of time where there is no work planned to be executed (therefore no planned performance), the actual performance cannot be compared against a reference.

An Alternative Approach: Earned Schedule

An alternative approach to measure time performance under EVM has been proposed based on the concept of ES. Basically, this approach converts the metrics PV and EV in to the time axis in the following way:

- PV is converted into AT – this is the time planned to have elapsed in the project to date, or alternatively the *time consumed* in the project.

- EV is converted into Earned Schedule – this is the time that should have elapsed considering the actual work accomplished.

By comparing the difference between Earned Schedule (time allocated in the plan for the work accomplished) and AT (time actually consumed, allocated for the work planned to date), a variance can be calculated called Time Variance (TV) = Earned Schedule (ES) – AT, as illustrated in Figure 8.7.

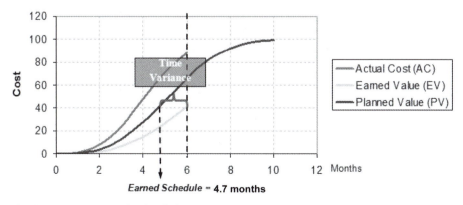

Figure 8.7   Earned schedule

In this simple example, six months elapsed to date (AT) and about 65 units of work should have been accomplished (PV). However, only 40 units of work were actually accomplished (EV). According to the plan, this amount of work accomplishment was due by month 4.7 (this is the ES value). Or in other words, it took six months to execute work that was planned to be executed in 4.7 months and therefore the project is behind schedule by 1.3 months – this is the TV.

A first appearance of the concept of TV calculated in this way dates back to 1990, in a book by John Nicholas (*Managing Business and Engineering Projects*, Prentice-Hall), and where the concept of ES is also present (although not under this name).

More recently, the use of EVM metrics based on this approach has deserved greater attention – the reader may wish to refer to the following website for more information and references: http://www.earnedschedule.com/. This approach suggests the following alternative metrics calculated in the time axis as opposed to the work volume (budget) axis:

- $SV(t) = ES - AT$. This is the concept of TV in Nicholas's book (1990);

- $SPI(t) = ES/AT$.

The first merit of this approach is that the problem of SPI floating towards the value of 1 in scenarios of early or late completion is resolved. Some of the main proponents of this approach also suggest that the Earned Schedule-based indicators also provide better predictions about the future project completion date.

Considering our previous example, Figure 8.8 shows the behaviours of the SPI(t) indicator, showing that after the completion date performance continues to be measured in a more consistent manner. The final value is consistent with the final result: the project was initially planned to be executed in ten months but it took 12.5 months to complete the work. Therefore, each month on average only produced 80% of the planned work (that is, $10/12.5 = 0.8$) and therefore more time was needed to complete the project. This is the final value for SPI(t) as follows:

- $SPI(t) = ES/AT = 10 \text{ months}/12.5 \text{ months} = 0.8$.

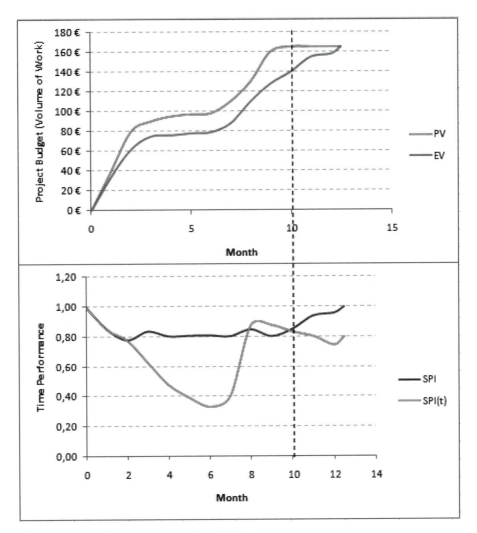

Figure 8.8   The final value for SPI(t)

While the pattern of variation of the new indicator seems to be sensitive to periods of time where the intensity of the work rate is planned to be low (that is, between months 2 and 8), its behaviour is certainly more consistent in the late completion period than the conventional SPI indicator.

In scenarios of early finishes, this new version of SPI also seems to maintain a consistent behaviour as shown in the following figure. It also corrects the final value of SPI, since although it may appear to have the same value, by month 8.33 when the work is completed the scenario is as follows:

- PV = 140;

- EV = 165;

- SPI = 140/165 = 1.18;

- SPI(t) = 10/8.33 = 1.2.

As it can be seen, the final value of the conventional SPI is not the same as SPI(t) (Figure 8.9). As already mentioned before, in an early finish the final value of conventional SPI might not be correct, which is the case in this example. The final time performance is in fact 20% above the planned performance (that is, 10 months of work were done in 8.33 months).

While the ES approach seems to resolve the problem of conventional SPI, it also presents at least two issues:

a) It seems to be very sensitive to periods of time where the planned work rate is slow. For example:

- project Planned Duration = 10 months;

- planned work (PV) by month 3 = $100;

- planned work (PV) by month 5 = $105;

  - AT = 5 months;
  - EV = $100;
  - ES = 3 months (time where PV = current EV);
  - SV(t) = -2 months;
  - SV = -$5;
  - SPI(t) = ES/AT = 3/5 = 0.6 = 60%;
  - SPI = EV/PV = 100/105 = 0.95 = 95%

So, the SPI(t) indicates a very low level of performance of 60%, whereas in reality only about 5% less work was actually accomplished than planned for the current date (that is, 100 units of actual work, against 105 units of planned work).

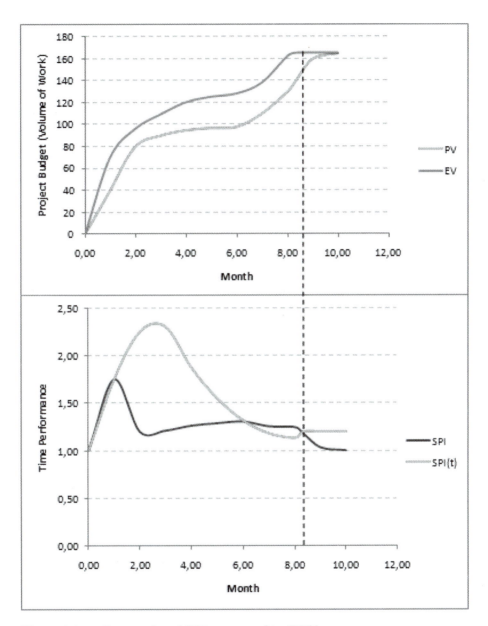

Figure 8.9 **Conventional SPI compared to SPI(t)**

b)   The fundamental meaning of time performance is changed, shifting the focus from 'how much work is behind/ahead of schedule' into 'how much time is the project behind/ahead of schedule'. In the simple example presented above one can confirm that the project is behind schedule by two months – but what is the real meaning of that measure? It means that the progress we currently achieved in the project (100 units of work) should have been achieved according to the plan two months ago. So one could say that this is 'equivalent' to a scenario where the work planned for the last two months was not accomplished (the project would have been paused for the last two months). While this is correct, the amount of work planned for those two months is as little as $5, representing less than 5% of the planned work (that is, 5/105). Therefore, these two months of delay represent a small volume of work and most likely are very easy to recover. Therefore, time variation during the project might not be as meaningful as volume variation in regards to appreciating the real size of a schedule performance problem. A recognised merit of EVM in measuring schedule performance is the focus on the volume of work behind schedule, which in practice is the real size of the problem in a late project: how much extra work do we need to fit into the remaining future time in order to complete the project on schedule? The answer is: the amount of work currently behind schedule (that is, SV). By focusing on the volume of work, the conventional SPI does have a merit over the ES alternative, by focusing closer to the cause of the delay as opposed to the delay itself. Time variation, that is TV or SV(t), is intuitive and useful information for the stakeholders, but a complete and more exhaustive appreciation of schedule performance must look into the volume of work behind schedule – the real problem that, if overcome by executing that work in the available time, will consequently eliminate the time delay (effect). Conventional SPI and SV relate and measure the size of that problem – how serious is the time delay? How much volume of work is within the current time delay? What does the current time delay represent in terms of work that needs to be recovered?

The author has developed another alternative to the calculation of SPI which on the one hand resolves the problems with the early and late finishes, while preserving the original focus of time performance on the volume of work ahead or behind schedule.

An Alternative Approach: Modified Schedule Performance Index

The alternative approach presented here was the result of various years of experience in implementing EVM in the field in a wide range of different projects and environments. It was also the result of academic research conducted by the author over the period of several years in the field of project management, using computer simulation models (System Dynamics Modelling – see Rodrigues 2001).

The approach proposed for a modified version of the SPI indicator is inspired by the laws of physics, where time performance can be related to the concept of velocity as follows:

- velocity (physics) = distance (km)/time (hours);

- velocity (project) = work units accomplished/Time Elapsed;

- SPI (time performance) = Actual Velocity/Planned Velocity (modified version of SPI).

Where:

- Actual Velocity = actual work accomplished (EV)/Time Elapsed;

- Planned Velocity = work planned to be accomplished (PV)/Time Elapsed.

And hence:

- SPI(modified) = (EV/Time Elapsed)/(PV/Time Elapsed).

And therefore SPI(m) = EV/PV = SPI (conventional).

This reasoning inspired by physics (where distance = work accomplished) leads us to the conventional SPI formula, so what is new? In the first place, this indicates that the volume-based SPI is consistent with the principles of time performance in physics.

It is irrefutable that the velocity of work accomplishment should equal the work accomplished to date divided by the Time Elapsed. Likewise, it is also irrefutable that the time performance measured in relative terms should be the ratio between the Actual Velocity and the Planned Velocity. So, let us consider our example again:

- project budget = $1,000:

  - baseline completion date = 5 months;

  - time now = 4 months;

  - PV (planned work) = $700 (that is, 700 units of work);

  - EV (actual work accomplished) = $500 (500 units of work);

  - Planned Velocity = PV/4 months = $700/4 months = 175 units of work/month;

  - Actual Velocity = EV/4 months = $500/4 months = 125 units of work/month;

  - SPI(m) = Actual Velocity/Planned Velocity = 125/175 = 0.71 = 71%;

  - SPI = EV/PV = 500/700 = 0.71 = 71%.

In summary, this project is being executed at a work rate (velocity) that is 71% of the originally planned work rate.

While this formula seems to produce the same result as the conventional SPI, in the cases of late finish and early finish the behaviour is different.

THE CASE OF A LATE FINISH

Let us consider our previous example:

- project budget = $1,000:

  - baseline completion date = 5 months;

  - time now = 10 months;

- PV (planned work) = $1,000 (that is, 1,000 units of work);

- EV (actual work accomplished) = $950 (950 units of work);

- Planned Velocity = $1,000/5 months = $200/month;

- Actual Velocity = $950/10 months = $95/month;

- SPI (modified) = ($95/month)/($200/month) = 0.475 = 47.5%;

- SPI (conventional) = EV/PV = 950/100 = 0.95 = 95%.

The modified SPI(m) indicates a time performance of 47.5%, well below the 95% given by the conventional SPI. This scenario also reveals the cause of the inconsistency with the conventional SPI in a late finish: when time moves beyond the baseline completion date the denominator for Actual Velocity and Planned Velocity is no longer the same and therefore the ratio of the work rates (planned and actual) can no longer be calculated as the ratio of EV/PV.

This leads us to a formula relating the modified SPI and the conventional SPI in a situation of a late finish:

- SPI(m) = SPI x (Time Elapsed/Planned Duration).

Where:

- correction factor = Time Elapsed/Planned Duration;

- when EV = PV (all work done and completion date elapsed);

- SPI(m) = Time Elapsed/Planned Duration.

The behaviour of SPI(m) in a situation of a late finish is illustrated in Figure 8.10.

As it can be observed, SPI(m) behaves like SPI(conventional) until the baseline completion date. After that point onwards, it does not float towards the value of 1 and it exhibits a consistent behaviour.

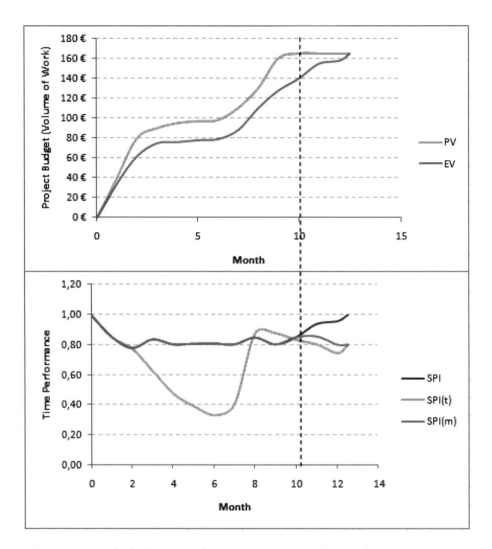

Figure 8.10   The behaviour of SPI(t) in the case of a late finish

It can also be observed that during the planned period SPI(m) seems to be robust against scenarios of low work intensity, unlike the SP(t) indicator based on ES.

In the period of delay, SPI(m) also shows a different performance than the SPI(t) indicator, although at the end of the project both will show exactly the same value (as can be demonstrated mathematically).

By looking at the whole period of project execution, the SPI(m) indicator seems to exhibit a more stable and consistent behaviour, closer to the real final value than the SPI(t) indicator, which seems to be more sensitive and unstable. This may have a significant impact on the quality of these indicators as predictors of the final completion date during project execution.

The SPI(m) indicator also retains the perspective on the volume of work accomplished which, as argued earlier, is more relevant than the time perspective. By comparing again with the laws of physics, we can consider the examples of a Formula 1 race versus a cycling race. Is the meaning of a five-seconds delay the same in both cases? Clearly not: five seconds in Formula 1 racing represents a significant distance (metres = volume of work) which generally is not easy to recover, whereas five seconds of delay in cycling racing can be meaningless because it represents a short distance between the two competitors. Likewise, in a project, a one-month delay can sometimes represent less than a one-week delay in terms of amount of work that needs to be recovered in the remaining future.

For information, the actual values that generated the figures for the late finish scenario are shown in Table 8.1.

Table 8.1   Figures for the scenario

Time	PV	EV	SPI(m)	ES	SPI(t)	SPI
0	0	0	1.00	0	1.00	1.00
1	40	34	0.85	0.85	0.85	0.85
2	80	62	0.78	1.55	0.78	0.78
3	90	75	0.83	1.875	0.63	0.83
4	95	76	0.80	1.9	0.48	0.80
5	97	78	0.80	1.95	0.39	0.80
6	98	79	0.81	1.975	0.33	0.81
7	110	88	0.80	2.8	0.40	0.80
8	130	110	0.85	7.00	0.88	0.85
9	160	128	0.80	7.9	0.88	0.80
10	165	140	0.85	8.33	0.83	0.85
11	165	155	0.85	8.83	0.80	0.94
12	165	158	0.80	8.93	0.74	0.96
12.5	165	165	0.80	10.00	0.80	1.00

THE CASE OF AN EARLY FINISH

Let us again consider our previous example:

- project budget = $1,000:

    - baseline completion date = 5 months;

    - time now = 4 months;

    - PV (planned work) = $700 (that is, 700 units of work);

    - EV (actual work accomplished) = $1,000 (100 units of work);

    - Planned Velocity = $1,000/5 months = $200/month;

    - Actual Velocity = $1,000/4 months = $250/month;

    - SPI (modified) = ($250/month)/($200/month) = 1.25 = 125%;

    - SPI (conventional) = EV/PV = 1,000/700 = 1.43 = 143%.

Again, the SPI(m) provides a different time performance value than the conventional SPI. It should be noted that when the work is completed earlier, the Planned Velocity should not be calculated as PV/Time Elapsed, but instead it should be calculated as the Budget at Completion (BAC)/Planned Duration (that is, the whole work divided by the Planned Duration). Therefore, when we compare the Actual Velocity against the Planned Velocity we are comparing against 1,000 units of work in five months ($200/month) and not against 700 units of work in four months – in fact, if we were to freeze the value of conventional SPI once the whole project work is completed, we would incorrectly conclude for a final time performance of 143%. This would also be the result of SPI(m) if we were not to look at the whole project once the work is completed.

The behaviour of SPI(m) in a situation of an early finish is illustrated in Figure 8.11. The conclusions are similar to the scenario of a late finish, where it can be seen that SPI(m) will not float towards one, nor it will give an incorrect final value as the conventional SPI would do if we were to freeze its value at the moment where the project was completed.

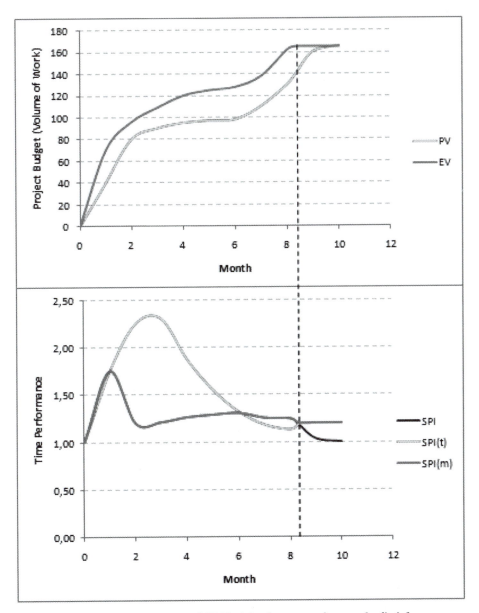

Figure 8.11   The behaviour of SPI(m) in the case of an early finish

For information, the actual values that generated the figures for the early finish scenario are shown in Table 8.2.

Table 8.2   **An extended EVM model for time management using the modified SPI**

Time	PV	EV	SPI(m)	ES	SPI(t)	SPI
0	0	0	1.00	0	1	1.00
1	40	70	1.75	1.8	1.75	1.75
2	80	96	1.20	4.5	2.25	1.20
3	90	109	1.21	6.9	2.31	1.21
4	95	120	1.26	7.5	1.88	1.26
5	97	125	1.29	7.8	1.55	1.29
6	98	128	1.31	7.9	1.32	1.31
7	110	138	1.25	8.3	1.18	1.25
8	130	162	1.25	9.1	1.13	1.25
8.33	140	165	1.20	10	1.20	1.18
9	160	165	1.20		1.20	1.03
10	165	165	1.20		1.20	1.00

The modified version of SPI proposed in this chapter creates the opportunity to develop an enhanced model of EVM for the purpose of time management. In particular, it is possible to answer the following questions:

a)   Given the current time performance level, what is the likely completion date if this level is maintained?

b)   Given an expected future time performance, what is the likely completion date for the project?

c)   What is the future time performance required to complete the project on a specific date?

•   If future performance needs to be increased, what is the required overall increase of in resource capacity?

•   If future performance can be decreased, what is the overall possible decrease in resource capacity?

•   If overall resource capacity is to be increased or decreased for the remainder of the project, what will be the impact on the likely project completion date?

d)   If the current time performance is below the planned level, resource capacity is maintained and the original completion date is imposed, what is the likely scope reduction?

e)   If a given completion date is imposed, and an expected future time performance is assumed, what will be the likely impact on scope?

In order to answer all these important management questions, a mathematical model equipped with a set of formulae was developed by the author as an extension to the standard EVM model – the EVM Strategic Model (EVM-SM™) which is described in a forthcoming book. This model was developed in the field through practical applications in various types of projects and in different industries.

A very important aspect of this EVM-based time management model is that it provides essential support to project risk management. In particular, the calculation of the required increase in the future time performance in order to complete the project on the original completion date is an effective indicator of the *schedule feasibility risk*. For example, if the future performance needs to be twice the planned level (that is, 100% increase, for example, executing two months of work in each remaining month) and such increase is known to be very unlikely (either based on expert judgement or even better on historical information), then the remaining schedule is most likely not feasible to attain and consequently the time risk is very high. If on the other hand, the performance increase is feasible (for example, a +10% increase) but the required resource capacity is not available, the time risk will also be very high. By confronting the project manager with the assumptions behind a *desired* schedule recovery, time risks can be identified earlier in the project, both for the project completion date and also for intermediate project milestones. The impact on the scope of the time risk can also be calculated as an overall scope reduction in percentage.

But will all this be just mathematics? No. All of these concepts translate into real world practice if properly applied. Let us briefly consider a real life example that I have been through recently.

A REAL LIFE EXAMPLE: USING SPI(M) FOR RISK MANAGEMENT

A medium-sized infrastructure construction project was scheduled for 12 months with a 25 million euro budget. What happened? Well the project started at a good pace in the first three months but after that SPI started to drop towards 0.5 and it stabilised at that level for the next three months, an overall history of six months corresponding to an SPI of 0.5 (50% of time performance). Particular and specific engineering-based explanations were given by the contractor as to why the problem had occurred (all of which were external, out of management reach, and with a hint of 'acts of God'). Technical solutions were always presented alongside the problems for recovery in the following month. But month after month, SPI never increased ... it maintained its value with a slight deterioration. By the eighth month, the client management finally confronted the contractor with the persistent trend, with a SPI of 0.47 – less than half of the planned work had been accomplished. What happened? Finally, a three-month delay was admitted by the contractor, for a partial relief of the client as after all the impact did not seem too bad given the circumstances. But was this partial recovery likely?

As external consultants we made use of the EVM-SM™ model by focusing on simple mathematics inspired (as previously described) in the laws of physics. First, by month eight the contractor claimed the initial schedule proposed by the client in the contract was infeasible. By looking at the original schedule, the current remaining scope had been planned to be executed in a period of time that implied a 2.5 million euro/month work rate – this was claimed by the contractor to be unrealistic given the characteristics of the scope and the project environment. As we looked into the recovery plan proposed by the contractor implying a three-month delay, and by looking at the current status of the project, the work rate implied was of three million euro/month, greater than the initially proposed schedule for the exact same scope. An unrealistic compressed schedule explained the poor past performance (that is, an 'invalid' baseline), but the recovery plan looked even more unrealistic. The client's management controller informed us that there was no historical evidence from past projects of work being executed at such an accelerated rate of three million euro/month. So, how was the contractor going to increase its overall resource capacity by over 50% (SPI(m) based calculations)? Well, the contractor informed us that, (to the dismay of the client), of course while the infrastructure would be fully operational in its 'essential features' a 'certain portion' of the scope would have to be postponed for a second phase. But what, and how much scope would have to be cut?

It can be seen that with simple calculations based on SPI(m) it was possible to uncover the scope impact from the time risk of the recovery plan and thereby the otherwise implicit assumptions were discussed before a feasible solution was agreed. On the other hand, had the early warnings of SPI been heard by month 4 then most likely the project would have followed a different and better course towards completion.

The use of aggregate EVM time performance indicators (namely SPI) has often been the subject of criticisms due to disregarding the details of the schedule and its critical paths and task floats. The fundamental mistake in this type of comparative analysis is that two different perspectives (bottom-up versus top-down) developed for different purposes (and which should be complementary), are being compared as if they were supposed to work at the same level of detail and perspective. The Critical Path Analysis (CPA) is grounded on a detailed perspective and provides a bottom-up estimation approach, certainly with the well-known merits of this type of approach. On the other hand, EVM works at the aggregate level and delivers a top-down estimation approach, a paradigm also with its own merits (for example, parametric cost models). So oranges are being compared against apples. In regards to time estimation, top-down techniques are known to be more reliable for the short-term future and less reliable for the longer-term (due to the intrinsic exponential growth of uncertainty in the detail level as we look into the far future). Top-down techniques provide the complementary view. Based on aggregation of results and high-level patterns, they deliver a more stable and consistent estimate for the long-term future and less granularity for the short term. Using both top-down and bottom-up techniques to complement one another, seems to be the intelligent way that capitalises on the best of both worlds.

Conclusions

This chapter discussed the problem of the shortcomings of the conventional SPI indicator in the EVM method as a reliable time performance indicator. The alternative method of evaluating time performance based on the concept of ES was also discussed and it was confirmed that it resolves the limitations of the conventional SPI indicator but it also changes the perspective and meaning of the time performance concept, shifting the perspective away from the cause of the delays (volume of work behind schedule) to the delay itself (amount of time behind schedule). An alternative method for calculating SPI – herein referred to as 'modified SPI', or simply SPI(m) – which preserves the original and valuable perspective of 'work volume', was proposed by the author and it has been demonstrated that it retains the merits of the work volume approach while resolving the limitations of the conventional SPI. This finding was based on over ten years of experience of using EVM in various different projects and organisational environments, plus several years of academic research based on computer simulation. The use of the proposed improved version of SPI, the SPI(m), has been successfully delivered over the last eight years in various real life projects. This finding is also important as it has a major impact on the potential of SPI to be used as a reliable predictor of the trend for the project completion date throughout execution and early in the project, as well as its potential to support effectively risk management.

Acknowledgements

The author would like express his gratitude to Mr Graham Muggeridge, from PMO Projects UK, for his exhaustive review of this chapter. I would also like to thank Professor Darren Dalcher, Director for the National Centre for Project Management, who challenged me to write this chapter, and to Mr Kym Henderson and Mr Wayne Abba for their encouragement and feedback. Also, special thanks to Mr David Pells and to PM Forum for publishing this work.

Further Reading

Abba, Wayne (1986, November–December). 'Cost/Schedule Control Systems Criteria White Paper.' *Program Manager* 15:45–47.

Abba, Wayne (2008, Fall). 'The Trouble with Earned Schedule.' *The Measurable News*, pp. 28–30.

Henderson, Kym (2003, Summer). 'Earned Schedule: A Breakthrough Extension to Earned Value Theory? – A Retrospective Analysis of Real Project Data.' *The Measurable News*, pp. 13–23.

Nicholas, John (1990). *Managing Business and Engineering Projects: Concepts and Implementation*. New Jersey: Prentice Hall.

Rodrigues, Alexandre (2001). 'The Application of System Dynamics to Project Management: An Integrated Methodology (SYDPIM).' PhD Dissertation Thesis. Department of Management Science, University of Strathclyde.

9

Spiritual Inspiration
Inspiration in Teams: Searching for a New Intelligence

Darren Dalcher

How do teams work together? What motivates them and leads them to success? Indeed, can project managers inspire teams?

Teams are formed when individuals are thrown together and given a set of challenges to overcome. Sometimes the individuals are selected on the basis of capabilities, or competences, but often they are not. The team is then expected to coalesce and ultimately perform at some higher level that feeds on the synergies that emerge when the parts come together to make the team. So how do teams become inspired?

To answer this we need to take a step back. Individuals in a team can be characterised through a set of capabilities. Traditional project management is considered to be rational and is therefore focused on intellectual aspects and skills, such as abstract thought, reasoning and planning. In recent years, the focus on IQ has been augmented by the discussion of the role of emotional intelligence (measured as EQ) in projects. Emotional intelligence in project management adds the interpersonal skills to the technical and problem-solving capabilities that already exist. EQ thus enables managers to assess their capabilities in dealing with 'softer' aspects such as stakeholders, relationships, self-awareness, social awareness, influencing, power and politics.

The combination of IQ and EQ can explain why we need to combine technical skills and rational intelligence with emotional awareness and interpersonal skills to deliver projects successfully. But what can account for inspired teams, with energy and enthusiasm? Clearly recognition of the needs of individuals can motivate and even inspire, but is it sufficient to explain the inspired performance of some teams?

Research in psychology has also focused on SQ, the Spiritual Quotient, or spiritual intelligence. SQ focuses on the emergent spiritual intelligence which is built on cognitions, beliefs, perceptions and intuitions that define the spiritual capital of a group or individual. They can account for a sense of camaraderie, a feeling of special mission or an inspired commission. Spiritual intelligence is associated with the tendency to inspire creativity, or innovation and encourage moral, ethical and responsible behaviour. It can also account for motivating influences in an individual or a group.

Leadership models increasingly focus on spiritual aspects and the role of spiritual intelligence, while many multinational corporations such as Nokia, Shell, Coca Cola and Starbucks invest in encouraging, measuring and improving spiritual intelligence. It is worth emphasising that SQ need not necessarily be connected to religion but could instead be linked to higher morals and principles, while featuring aspects such as humility and a greater awareness of a participant's role and position in the context of the wider world.

The chapter by Dr Judi Neal and Alan Harpham explores the role of spirituality in project teams. They further discuss the benefits to the organisation and highlight the approaches that can be utilised in leading teams in a spiritual manner. The material draws on their book *Spirituality and Project Management* published by Gower in the Advances in Project Management book series.

The authors make an important contribution to the discipline by opening up a discussion on the skills required in inspiring teams. Ethical leadership is also recognised as a crucial area in many corporations and it is encouraging to see an informed discussion developing within the project management community. The book attempts to open up new areas for exploration which extend beyond the traditional remit of project management knowledge and thus deserves credit for fostering much needed discussion and reflection in the discipline. The search for new types of intelligence will continue and many debates will no doubt ensue. Through this type of exploration and discussion the discipline can start addressing questions related to what brings teams together and how to inspire them into higher achievements. Regardless of the belief system or religious and ethical doctrine of a project manager, the ability to inspire, guide, motivate and embrace 'spirited teams' should attract project managers to this arena and invite them to consider a new perspective on performance, purpose and achievement.

Spirituality in Project Management Teams

Judi Neal and Alan Harpham

All human beings are spiritual beings so there is potential for collective spiritual energy whenever people come together. As Jesus said, 'Where two or three are gathered in my name, there I am' (Matthew 18:20). Hindus gather together in Satsang, or spiritual community, as an important part of evolving in their consciousness. Native Americans gather in Wisdom Councils for spiritual guidance about major decisions that affect the tribe and future generations. All wisdom traditions have spiritual practices incorporating a group of people coming together for some higher purpose.

A spiritual approach to project management team development and leadership benefits individual team members in their own spiritual development. Project stakeholders also benefit, because team members are more committed, inspired and effective in implementing the processes needed for success.

There are five approaches that a project manager might consider when leading project teams in a spiritual way:

1. alignment

2. spiritual leadership

3. esprit de corps

4. communication

5. creativity

Each approach will be described briefly, with examples of activities and processes you might use in your project team.

Alignment: Aligning Vision, Meaning and Purpose at the Team Level

In order to align vision, meaning and purpose within your project management team, you, as project manager, must first be clear about your own vision for the project, and what its meaning and purpose is for you in your own life and work (Barrett 2006). It is essential to communicate your vision and to be willing to share on a personal level how this project provides meaning and purpose to you. You also need to communicate to your team what the meaning and purpose of the project is to the stakeholders.

The next step is to create alignment within the team and, in order to do this, you must be open to having your own vision, meaning and purpose enhanced by what others in the team have to say. One process for creating alignment is to bring people together for an Alignment Session and to ask them each to write a brief story about a past project that provided a strong sense of meaning and purpose. Stories are a time-honoured tradition for evoking spiritual wisdom. Next, put them in small groups of three to five people to share their stories, and ask them to listen for themes and similarities. Have people collect these themes on flip charts or through decision software. Once each group has completed their list of themes regarding meaning and purpose, ask for two or three volunteers to tell the entire group a little bit about their projects where they felt a strong sense of meaning and purpose. List all the themes on a white board or other data collection method that is visible to everyone. Finally, lead a discussion with full participation to discuss each person's vision for the project and how this project can create a shared, collective meaning and purpose for the team as a whole.

Spiritual Leadership: Seeing Oneself as a Servant Leader to the Team and Being Committed to Helping Each Team Member be a Servant Leader to Others

One of the most popular of the many different models of spiritual leadership is Servant Leadership based on a framework developed by Robert Greenleaf, a retired executive from AT&T. He developed this model after reading

Hermann Hesse's spiritual tale, *The Journey to the East* (Hesse 1932). Greenleaf (1977) offers this test of whether someone is a Servant Leader:

> *Do those served grow as persons; do they while being served become healthier, wiser, freer, more autonomous, more likely themselves to become servants?*

Larry Spears, former Director of the Greenleaf Center for Servant Leadership, identified ten characteristics of a Servant Leader, several of which are quite spiritual in nature. For example, one characteristic is awareness, which is central to all major religious traditions (Spears 1998). Contemplative practices such as prayer, meditation and journaling are powerful tools for self-awareness. As a project manager, we recommend that you consider taking on or deepening some kind of contemplative practice.

Another characteristic of spiritual leaders is commitment to the growth of people, with a belief that people have an intrinsic value beyond their tangible contribution as workers. This is also one of key characteristics of an effective project manager. Leaders who exhibit this characteristic are high in spiritual intelligence. You might wish to consider taking the Spiritual Intelligence Survey as a way of learning about your spiritual strengths and areas of growth as a leader (Wigglesworth 2010).

Jody Fry (2003, 2005) has done extensive research on spiritual leadership and has developed a causal model demonstrating the relationship between (1) spiritual leadership values, attitudes and behaviours; (2) the needs of followers for spiritual survival; and (3) organisational outcomes. His research shows that vision, hope/faith, and altruistic love lead to organisational commitment, productivity, ethical and spiritual well-being, and corporate social responsibility. For team leaders who wonder if there is a business case for spiritual leadership, Fry's work is well worth reading, and can inspire you to be the kind of spiritual leader your heart may be calling you to be.

Esprit de Corps: Understanding and Honouring the Collective Spirit of the Team

Each of us has at one time or another been on a project team where there was an incredible sense of esprit de corps. Esprit de corps is defined as 'the common spirit existing in the members of a group and inspiring enthusiasm, devotion, and strong regard for the honour of the group' (Merriam-Webster online retrieved 30 August 2010). Literally it means 'spirit of the group'.

A team is a living system, and each living system has its own spirit. Just as we each have our own spirit and must consciously do things to nourish that spirit, a team must consciously do things to nourish the spirit of the team. Barry Heermann developed a programme called Team Spirit (1997) that incorporates organisational development practices, group dynamics processes and knowledge from the wisdom traditions of the world. Team Spirit has a six-phase Team Spirit Spiral with activities at every stage, all of which centre around service. Heermann and his colleagues have learned that teams with esprit de corps and high performance are distinguished by their focus on service to each other and to the customer or stakeholder. Therefore, to create more esprit de corps, we suggest that you have discussions with your project team about what service means to them and how they feel about the people who will be served by the project.

Communication: Including Non-traditional Communication Methods as Ways of Building Trust and Openness

All good project managers are very clear about traditional methods of communicating the goals of a project, the deliverables and the expectations about deadlines and costs. These are necessary, but not sufficient for leading project management teams from a more profound spiritual place. If you really want to tap into the spiritual energy and wisdom of a team, you will need to add some non-traditional communication methods to your skill set.

One of these communication methods you might want to experiment with is Bohmian Dialogue. This is a method of developing deeper self-awareness and team consciousness in a group of people, and does not have a specific agenda or task outcome. The purpose is to develop a deeper level of listening to the group's collective wisdom.

There are four principles of Bohmian Dialogue:

1.   The group agrees that no group-level decisions will be made in the conversation.

2.   Each individual agrees to suspend judgement in the conversation.

3.   As these individuals 'suspend judgement' they also simultaneously are as honest and transparent as possible.

4.   Individuals in the conversation try to build on other individuals' ideas in the conversation (Bohm et al. 2004).

Bohmian Dialogue is used when logic and analysis have run up against limitations and a project management team needs to create something it does not know how to do. This is a form of conversation that is meant to be generative rather than problem solving.

Creativity: Recognising that Inspiration Comes from Spirit, and Utilising Group Spiritual Practices from the Wisdom Traditions to Support Inspired Problem Solving

The word 'inspiration' comes from the Latin word '*spirare*', which means spirit, and also means breath. While much of project management is based on linear processes and time lines, there are many opportunities for creativity, especially early in the project. But creativity is also necessary when risk and uncertainty create unexpected turns of events (Cleden 2009).

One example of a spiritual practice that supports creativity is a team experience of walking the labyrinth. The labyrinth is a meditative tool for stimulating creativity and problem solving, and is used in organisations for providing a non-threatening way to demonstrate the positive use of spiritual practices in the workplace. The labyrinth is an ancient spiritual ritual common to cultures as varied as the Native Americans, Norwegians and fourteenth-century Catholic monks. It is a form of walking meditation where one walks on a circular path marked on the floor or the ground, beginning on the outside and gradually moving to the centre. After some time for reflection in the centre, the walker returns the same way, in contemplation, towards the outside of the labyrinth and to the exit (Neal and Miguez 2000). This process has been used for helping teams envision the future, solve difficult challenges with a project and make creative breakthroughs in design and implementation.

Overall, a spiritual approach to managing project teams can benefit both the organisation and the team members. There is a long history of leaders taking spiritual approaches to projects, and in more recent times, project managers are more explicitly implementing spiritual values and practices. Five approaches were described in this chapter and are offered in much greater detail in our book, *The Spirit of Project Management*. These five approaches are (1) alignment, (2) spiritual leadership, (3) esprit de corps, (4) communication and (5) creativity.

Each of these spiritual approaches has been used in project management teams, from small businesses to large organisations such as Scott Bader, Microsoft UK, Pfizer and Xerox. It is our hope that you will feel inspired to adopt one or more of these approaches in your project management team. If you wish to find consultants who can help you adapt any of the processes to your project team, feel free to contact the authors for recommendations of qualified people in your geographic area or your industry.

References

Barrett, Richard (2006). *Building a Values-driven Organization: A Whole System Approach to Cultural Transformation*. Cambridge, MA: Butterworth-Heinemann.

Bohm, David, Lee, Nichol and Senge, Peter (2004). *On Dialogue*. London: Routledge.

Cleden, David (2009). *Managing Project Uncertainty*. Farnham: Gower Publishing.

Fry, Louis W. (2003). 'Toward a Theory of Spiritual Leadership.' *Leadership Quarterly* 14:693–727.

Fry, Louis W. (2005). 'Toward a theory of ethical and spiritual well-being and corporate social responsibility through spiritual leadership'. In: Robert A. Giacalone, Carol L. Jurkiewicz (eds), *Postive Psychology in Business Ethics and Corporate Responsibility*. Greenwich, CT: Information Age Publishing.

Greenleaf, Robert K. (1977). *Servant Leadership: A Journey into the Nature of Legitimate Power and Greatness*. Mahwah, NJ: Paulist Press.

Heermann, Barry (1997). *Building Team Spirit: Activities for Inspiring and Energizing Teams*. NY: McGraw-Hill.

Hesse, Herman (1932). *Journey to the East*. Germany: Samuel Fischer.

Matthew 18:20 (2009). *New International Version*. Grand Rapids, MI: Zondervan.

Merriam-Webster online retrieved 30 August 2010.

Neal, Judi and Harpham, Alan (2012). *The Spirit of Project Management*. Farnham: Gower Publishing.

Neal, Judi and Miguez, J. (1999). *The Labyrinth: A Life-giving Tool for Organizations*. Philadelphia, PA: Eastern Academy of Management.

Spears, Larry (ed.) (1998). *The Power of Servant-Leadership*. San Francisco, CA: Jossey-Bass.

Wigglesworth, Cindy (2010). 'Spiritual Intelligence: Why it Matters.' Recovered from: http://daveatwood.com/uploads/2/8/4/4/2844368/spiritual_intelligence__emotional_intelligence_2011.pdf (accessed 5 December 2013).

10

Ethics

Project Ethics and Professionalism: The Making of a Profession?

Darren Dalcher

Our last chapter focused on the oft ignored spiritual aspect of teams. In this instalment we shift attention to another soft and fuzzy area, the ethical dimension and its role in professional project management.

Mirroring the corporate culture, the area of ethics is assuming greater importance in project management with most professional associations establishing professional codes. With an increased focus on the professionalisation of the discipline there is an implicit expectation that project managers will behave in ethical and professional ways, discharging their duties in a moral and responsible fashion. Many of the codes hint that potential breaches may result in exclusion or further sanctions, suggesting that there is a clear position that can be evaluated and judged by an external agency. In reality, right and wrong are not absolute positions that are always easy to define and address. Ethical decision making implies grappling with shades of grey and trying to make sense of alternative positions, expectations and values.

The fifth edition of the *APM Body of Knowledge* (*APM BOK*) features 52 topics required for the successful management of projects. The very last of these topics describes the area of 'Professionalism and Ethics'. The *APM BOK* makes it clear that individuals should follow standards of professional ethics and behave 'appropriately'. It further explains that a project manager needs to act in equity, good faith and good conscience with due regard for the interests of the organisation or client. Ethical requirements form an integral part of professional behaviour and require fundamental understanding of expectations, moral values and legal boundaries thereby necessitating managers to display morally, legally and socially appropriate manners of behaving and working. Indeed, the International Project Management Association (IPMA) Competence Baseline clearly places ethics amongst the required behavioural competences of a project manager.

It would be reassuring, albeit simplistic, to be able to reduce ethical conflict and professional decisions to rights and wrongs. The law is mandatory, offering a framework for determining what is acceptable, so that one is obliged to obey the principles enshrined in legal definitions. Note, however, that even in a legal context differing interpretations and precedents can sometimes redefine right and wrong. Ethics extends beyond the mandatory dictates of the legal system into the discretionary world of choice. The basis for ethics is the focus on values held by different individuals and groups and the ability to reconcile different sets.

Given the subjective nature of values and the strength with which they are held, making choices becomes a complex and demanding task. Ethical dilemmas are often portrayed as dealing with different shades of grey as the choice is not between right or wrong, but between right and right (as seen from different perspectives and value systems). Professionals are expected to grapple with conflicting value and make informed, good enough decisions. In the course of making such decisions we continue to expect project professionals not to compromise the interests of the project, the interested parties, the organisations involved and society, whilst upholding their own personal values.

The chapter by Dr Haukur Ingi Jónasson and Dr Helgi Thor Ingason explores the position of project ethics from the perspective of the project manager. If project management becomes a profession, what are the implications on those practising it from an ethical perspective and what are the implications for professionalism? The material draws on their book *Project Ethics* published by Gower in the Advances in Project Management book series.

The authors make an important contribution to the discipline by opening up a discussion about professionalism and ethics. Ethics cannot be viewed as a simple competence existing in isolation that can be addressed or simplistically ticked in checklist. Instead it is a defining aspect and a guiding moral compass of a growing profession. Professionals need to embrace the concept and allow it to guide their professional actions. Whether we learn to address it will determine how we are all viewed in the future.

Project Ethics: The Critical Path to Development

Haukur Ingi Jónasson and Helgi Thor Ingason

The critical path is one of the fundamental concepts in traditional project management. In fact, the inception of the Critical Path Method (CPM) is sometimes considered to be a symbolic milestone; a starting point for the establishment of project management as a formal discipline. Traditionally, project management focused on time, cost and the quality of the project outcome. Understanding that certain tasks in the project work breakdown structure were more important than other tasks for delivering the project within a given timeframe, and being able to make calculations and identify those tasks, was a breakthrough. Identifying this critical path of tasks became an important management tool and symbolises the origin of project management as a sub-discipline of operation research.

But can we find other critical paths in projects? Can we identify paths that are even more important than the simple – or complex – system of tasks being connected in different ways along the project life cycle? Yes, we can. And over the last decade the project management community has focused considerably on other kinds of critical paths, namely the ever so critical paths of communication, leadership and the way people think, collaborate and operate. In the same way we, as individuals, strive to walk the critical path of good deeds throughout our lives, it can be argued that projects also have critical paths that don't have much to do with time and cost. The project manager and his/her team need to be able to identify appropriate ethical behaviour in their undertakings.

As project managers we are faced with different alternatives, different ways we can deal with difficult situations. Should we choose alternative

A or B? Alternative A will deliver the project on time and budget but we will have to compromise our perception of what is right and wrong and act in a way that opposes our moral standards. Alternative B means that we do the right thing according to our moral standards but we will not deliver the project on time and on budget. In this case we have to choose between the critical path of conventional project management and the critical path of our personal moral values. How can we make such a decision? Project ethics puts forward some tools and ways of thinking to help project managers in such a critical situation.

Being a Professional

Our basic understanding of the term profession is that a profession is founded upon educational training. The purpose of a profession is to supply a service for a monetary compensation. A professional is thus a member of a profession with certain attributes: a professional is typically academically qualified and traditionally has obtained a degree in a specialised field. He has specialised knowledge, experience and skills in his field. A professional is expected to have extensive competence in his particular profession. Being a professional means being trusted on the basis of professional competence and knowledge. Most professionals are thus held up to strict ethical and moral regulations. A professional has a positive attitude towards the profession and is loyal towards his client and very aware of his duty towards him. From this discussion, we can conclude that being a professional is not just a career path; it is a combination of education and training and includes a sense of morals and motivation.

The Competent Project Manager

Based on our general discussion of the term professional, we will now consider whether a project manager is a professional. A project manager is typically a person with a high level of education in a particular field. He may have studied project management at an academic level, through short courses or more extensive university programmes. He has learned project management by experience; by participating in projects, holding managerial roles and taking on the responsibility of project manager in different projects during his professional life. A project manager is someone who must take into account the interests of different parties in the project environment: clients, institutions, contractors and specialists to name a few. A project manager needs to be able to evaluate different interests and make decisions that are good and appropriate for the project, the client, society and himself. Project management associations around the world have started certifying project managers, thereby confirming that individuals have certain measurable knowledge and experience. This development further substantiates that project management is a profession and defines in more specific terms what this profession entails.

Having established that project management is a profession, it is logical to ask what makes a good professional in the profession of project management? What is a competent project manager? Different project management associations have provided a wide range of answers to this question, but some answers have a lot in common. The International Project Management Association (IPMA) has described project management in terms of three main areas of competence that are required within this profession: technical, contextual and behavioural competences. **Technical competences** have to do with the traditional project management discipline, cost, time and quality management and a set of technical methods that are used to prepare and execute projects. **Contextual competences** have to do with the context of the project, its connection with its environment, the link between the project and the mother organisation through sponsorship, procedures, portfolio and programmes. **Behavioural competences** have to do with the way people act and behave, leadership, conflict, communication, personal development and numerous related things, including ethical aspects. Alternatively, the American Project Management Institute (PMI) defines project management in terms of nine knowledge areas: management of cost, time, scope, quality, human resources, risk, communication, procurement and integration.

These sources provide different versions of what it is to be a good project management professional; a competent project manager. They share some indicators, but IPMA gives more attention to aspects of human behaviour, relationships, communication and the way we act and react as human beings. Being a competent project manager in modern times is thus not only to be able to do the right thing and do things right; to plan a project and execute it on time, budget and quality. It also involves being able to understand the way the project is linked and related to its environment, its mother organisations and different institutions and interested parties. Last but not least, being a competent project manager is to understand your own strengths and weaknesses and the way you and other people act and react in different situations. A competent project manager is humble and respects other people's values, knowledge and opinions, and he understands the way we humans are a part of a larger whole and a sensitive harmony that can be influenced by a project. He also understands how projects are part of a much larger context of organisations and societies.

If project management as a discipline wants to move away from being a career path and become a respected profession in its own right, it will have to keep up with defining its professional virtues, duties and rights. Ethics cannot be defined as just one of the necessary competences of a project manager. Ethics rather defines the heart of the profession. There are many exciting paths to take, some are wide and easy paths that might generate loads of income while others are the narrow and more demanding paths of the qualified expert. In the future it is the professional project manager who will define the critical path of the prolific profession of project management.

11

Stakeholders
Can We Satisfy Project Stakeholders?

Darren Dalcher

Our last chapter featured the ethical and professional aspects of project management. The chapter made a case for professionalising the discipline of project management. The editorial introduction talked about ethical dilemmas and the need to balance perspectives and values. This subsequent chapter continues the theme by focusing in on project stakeholders.

The traditional emphasis on balancing time, cost and performance in projects is often described as inadequate. Indeed the successful delivery of benefits related to the project can often be translated as the fulfilment of the needs and expectations of stakeholders. As we extend the definition of success in projects, some contend that projects are required to meet all stakeholder expectations.

Balancing perspectives, expectations, needs and values is difficult to attain. Even more so when stakeholders groups are not fully identified or understood. If a stakeholder is anyone who may be impacted by a project, identifying all such concerned parties can be challenging especially at the outset. Moreover, being a stakeholder is self-legitimising to the extent that a declared interest in a project qualifies the claimant to become one. Therefore if project management is to embrace the satisfaction of all concerns and expectations of stakeholders, we may need to expand our scope of interest to include all parties who elect to join us in declaring an interest.

Needs, expectations and values adjust and shift during the duration of a project thereby creating a need to maintain active relationships with stakeholders in the long term. Where success equates with creating satisfied stakeholders, our ideas and theories related to how we identify, understand, sustain and satisfy stakeholders require a significant update.

The chapter by Dr Pernille Eskerod and Dr Anna Lund Jepsen sheds light on some of the changes that are required in managing and satisfying stakeholders. Given the increasing prominence of stakeholders in a relationship that extends beyond a single project, a clearer understanding of the motives and values of stakeholders can pave the way to longer-term success. The chapter identifies four major considerations that can be used to better understand and influence stakeholders, thereby offering new insights into the true complexity of stakeholder engagement.

The chapter can play an important part in reconceptualising and clarifying the role and impact of a stakeholder. It introduces new ideas such as the stakeholders adding a new dimension in considering actions, preferences, choices and motivation. The chapter draws on their book *Project Stakeholder Management* published by Gower in the Fundamentals of Project Management book series.

The authors provide fresh ideas and insights that will invigorate the thinking around stakeholder engagement and successful delivery. The new insights that promise to enrich and broaden our perspective borrow from strategic management and marketing as the authors endeavour to redefine our understanding of stakeholders, their needs and role. Ultimately, satisfying expectations presupposes an understanding of needs and preferences. As we strive to improve project management practices, a new and more meaningful understanding of the values and perspectives of stakeholders can begin to underpin new efforts to successfully deliver relevant business benefits and engage with stakeholders. While we may still need to prioritise and balance values and perspectives, we can do so with the benefit of greater visibility and perspective offered by the authors.

What Does the Project Stakeholder Value?

Pernille Eskerod and Anna Lund Jepsen

A project is a means to create value for stakeholders. This is a two-way street as contributions from the stakeholders are imperative to create the desired value. The existing project management literature offers advice on how to manage project stakeholders to enhance the likelihood that agreed upon deliverables will be delivered within time and budget by the project team. The literature is based on a notion of a stable environment in which both the project task and the stakeholders are 'manageable'. Today's projects, however, are often faced by unexpected changes in the environment. This means that the project representatives (the project sponsor, the project manager and the project team members) continuously need to adjust the project plan and thereby potentially affect the stakeholders. Further, many organisations desire sustaining relationships with their stakeholders. Only satisfied stakeholders will want to sustain their relationships and knowledge about their preferences is therefore necessary. Our claim is that the current literature on project stakeholder management is not well-suited for dealing with the challenges related to project stakeholder management facing today's project representatives as the understanding of project stakeholders' interests and value perception is not sufficiently unfolded. A clear understanding of the project stakeholder values may enable the project representatives to create better value for all stakeholders.

To better address project stakeholder values in a broad sense we suggest that the project management literature should be enriched by concepts, tools, and theories from (1) stakeholder management within the strategic management literature; and (2) consumer behaviour within the marketing literature.

With inspiration from these theoretical frameworks, four major considerations of each project stakeholder can be determined:

1   What is in it for Me, and What is Fair?

A stakeholder has a free will to decide whether to contribute to a certain project or not. In this decision-making process the stakeholder will consider the net satisfaction, that is, whether the anticipated benefits for the stakeholder are higher than the anticipated costs of contributing. However, research has shown that the stakeholder's willingness to contribute is influenced by his or her perception of fairness, that is, how project representatives approve of the way in which the project sponsor, the project manager and the project team members treat the stakeholders. The perception of fairness relates to the distribution of benefits among the stakeholders and how project processes take place, for example, whether the stakeholders are sufficiently involved in the decision making as well as informed properly in a timely manner. Further, ways of interaction are also taken into consideration in the fairness assessment, that is, do the project representatives interact with the stakeholders in a respectful way?

2   What is Appropriate for a Person Like Me in a Situation Like This?

Stakeholders make their decision as regards contribution in a social context. Therefore, the stakeholders also take into account what they believe they are supposed to do, that is, they consider 'what would a person like me do in a situation like this?'. Through interactions with their environment, the stakeholders have developed a certain understanding of their role and how others see them – a social self-image – and they act in a manner which they believe will support and sustain this image. This holds true for the project stakeholder's interactions with the project representatives but also with other stakeholders.

3   I Have My Own Stakeholders!

Classical project stakeholder management theory/guidelines emphasises the dual relationships between the project and each of the stakeholders. It can be tempting for the project representatives to see the project as the centre of the world as this helps focusing on accomplishing the project. It is important to remember, however, that the project may not be the centre of the world for the stakeholders and that each project stakeholder has his or her own stakeholders to relate to – and other stakeholders may be perceived as equally or even more important than the project representatives.

4   I Am the One Who Knows My Priorities!

When unexpected events happen in the project course, project representatives often need to make tradeoffs. If the project representatives don't know the considerations and priorities of the stakeholder, but only stick to their own priorities, the consequences of a change response may not be adequate to the interests and the values of the stakeholders. This is illustrated in the case example below.

CASE

The author (the stakeholder) of a well-known text book in project management who also was the publisher himself had gotten a new printing company (which undertakes the project) to print the ninth version of his book. Agreements on, for example, specifications, budget and deadlines were stated in a contract and everything seemed fine. A characteristic of the previous versions of the book was that the second half of the book was printed on yellow paper to emphasise that this half was not traditional text chapters but appendices presenting project management tools. This design was also chosen for this particular version. However, the printing company's supplier could not deliver yellow paper in time. The author was not informed about this problem. Shortly before the agreed upon deadline for the book deliverance, he received a message from the printing company saying that the book would be delayed due to the lack of yellow paper supply. As a result the book was not available in book stores for the semester start, resulting in a lot of frustrated students and professors; less revenue from the book sale; and the risk that the book would not be on next year's book lists. The author was very unhappy about the situation. 'Had they just contacted me,' he said, 'then I would have told them to print the appendices on white paper. To have the text book delivered in time for the semester start had my highest priority.'

The case example shows a situation in which none of the four considerations mentioned above were properly taken care of by the project representatives when the unexpected event occurred: (1) The author (the stakeholder) felt that he was not properly informed about the lacking supply. Neither was he involved in the tradeoff decision between time (delivering at the promised deadline) and specifications (delivering the book with white and yellow pages), which related to his perception of process fairness. (2) The author had delivered text books to students and professors for many years. He felt it was threatening for his image as a reliable book supplier that the book was not available in the book stores when needed. (3) The project representatives did not consider the core interests of the stakeholder's stakeholders, that is, the book stores, the students and the professors. (4) When the project representatives were faced with the need for making a tradeoff decision between time and specifications, they did what they found best themselves (if they considered the alternatives at all), without asking the stakeholder about his priorities.

Our message is this: An unexpected event occurred and the project representatives had to choose a change response. By not considering the stakeholder's considerations and value perception the project representatives did not minimise the damage. Instead they made it much worse than necessary. Stakeholder management has a lot to offer but must begin with a better understanding of what project stakeholders value.

12

Supply Chains
Managing Connected Supply Chains

Darren Dalcher

Should project managers learn to manage their suppliers?

Our last chapter focused on managing stakeholders with a particular emphasis on relationships and the achievement of priorities. It also highlighted a common situation where an individual stakeholder may have their own stakeholders that they need to keep engaged and involved. In this chapter we shift our focus to supply chains: networks that connect multiple suppliers and customers through complex webs of relationships. The relationships often involve chains of suppliers (and therefore chains of customers) that need to be managed and engaged.

Supply chains are all around us as they underpin the delivery of goods, products, services, finances or information. In a connected economy the networks that ensure timely delivery and connect suppliers and customers become more crucial to the successful operation and survival of companies, economies and countries. Project management texts often ignore the role of supply chains in projects as they take a temporal project-centric view of what needs to be delivered and what must be organised to ensure everything is in place.

In June 2008 the Supply Chain Council reported that according to their membership 'less than half of enterprises have established metrics and procedures for assessing and managing supply risks and organisations lack sufficient market intelligence, process, and information systems to effectively predict and mitigate supply chain risks'. The risks and the lack of established procedures in organisations concerned with supply chains may translate into a greater need in project-focused and project-based organisations where long-term relationships may be sacrificed in the interest of delivering outputs and outcomes according to project plans and schedules.

Indeed, as we start to consider the complexity of some of the chains linking suppliers with their own suppliers we can begin to imagine the potential vulnerabilities of our system of delivering results through projects. The assumption that resources will be available when needed suddenly depends on chains of conditions involving stakeholders we may not identify or recognise. The questions we need to ask are 'how do we start to build the infrastructure for managing complex supply chains?' and 'what basic building blocks are available in order to achieve that?'

The chapter by Dr Ron Basu offers some of the answers. It starts by identifying a number of critical chains that are relevant to successful project work. Indeed, it goes beyond looking at project delivery to include aspects of project planning as well as project integration. The three chains extend throughout the extended life cycle of a project, covering all activities between the proposal stage and project closure. The chapter identifies six supply chain configuration components and three integration components which apply to most projects.

The chapter provides the vocabulary and building blocks needed to consider the risks and issues associated with managing supply chains in projects. The chapter draws on Ron's book *Managing Project Supply Chains* published by Gower in the Advances in Project Management book series.

The author provides clear constructs and a framework for developing and addressing supply chains in projects. Understanding the chains that are needed to deliver the goods, services and products which underpin projects is crucial to developing a deeper understanding of the theory and practice of successful project management. In practice, we may never learn to manage our suppliers (and nor should we try to manage them), but we can make a good start by appreciating their chains, links, networks and priorities and focus on creating long-lasting relationships steeped in mutual understanding of concerns, constraints and chains.

Managing Project Supply Chains

Ron Basu

Introduction

The essential success criterion of a project is the timely, accurate to quality and cost-effective delivery of materials, systems and facilities. There are many stakeholders, contractors and suppliers involved in a project. In a major infrastructure scheme such as Heathrow Terminal 5 there are likely to be more than 100 key contractors and consulting firms. Thus, supply chain management methodologies and processes are crucial to ensuring that project resources are delivered as required.

In the context of a major project, supply chain management can experience additional risks appearing from the multiple tiers of suppliers and the intended linear process becomes unreliable. In order to minimise such non-linear project risks related to the project supply chain the basic concepts, skills and tools of supply chain management form essential support elements of project management.

Project Supply Chain Building Blocks

It is important that a 'Total Supply Chain Management approach' is applied and all the building blocks of the project supply chain are examined. If one concentrates exclusively on isolated areas, a false impression may be inevitable and inappropriate action taken. Our model for Total Supply Chain Management in projects comprises nine building block configurations in three streams, viz:

1. **Project planning chain**: In this stream the building blocks are dealing with project planning activities and the information flow. The building blocks in this stream are:

    — customer focus and stakeholders;

    — resources and time management;

    — procurement and supplier focus.

2.   **Project delivery chain**: Here, the building blocks relate to the project implementation and closure activities and physical flow of materials on site. The building blocks in this stream are:

    — supply management;

    — building and installation;

    — handover and closure.

3.   **Project integration**: In this group the building components of project supply chain are acting as the integrators of other building blocks as various stages of the project life cycle. The building components in this stream are:

    — systems and procedures;

    — regular reviews;

    — quality and performance management.

This model is illustrated in Figure 12.1. Each of the building blocks is briefly described below.

PROJECT PLANNING CHAIN

Customers exist both at the start and end of the supply chain. In a project supply chain a customer could be a sponsor, an investor or an end user. The basis of all supply chain planning and decisions is underpinned by the forecast of future demand created by customers. In all instances of a supply chain the first step is to forecast what the customer expectations will be in the future. It is recognised that a critical determinant of project success is agreeing the success criteria with key stakeholders, in addition to customers, before any design or planning activity. The demand forecast actually depends on project deliverables defined by the Product Breakdown Structure.

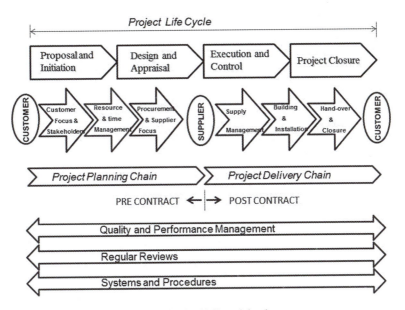

Figure 12.1   Project supply chain building blocks

A primary objective of supply chain management is to optimise the supply capacity to fulfil demand in time. One such process of optimisation is Enterprise Resource Planning (ERP) which has evolved from MRPII (Manufacturing Resource Planning). Number crunching is done using a computer system such as SAP R/3. The success of ERP in operations management is now being extended to project management.

In project management, Critical Path Scheduling and Earned Value Management (EVM) are popular tools for assigning resources and time. The planning processes are supported by software such as MS Project and Primavera. However the application of ERP in major projects is now assisting resources planning and procurement schedules and is interfaced with Enterprise Project Management (EPM) systems.

Project procurement is often considered the focal point of project supply chain and the supply chain manager is usually selected from a procurement background. The procurement activities in projects have two main subdivisions: the buying of materials and placing contracts with suppliers and contractors. Hence procurement and supplier focus are interconnected. The optimisation of internal capacity can be supplemented by buying in external capacity and resources.

For the project supply chain, the procurement of external capacity and resources could include construction materials, part built up assemblies, contracting out utilities and maintenance, hiring casual labour, selecting approved suppliers and outsourcing. The selection of appropriate or preferred suppliers should involve alternative and complementary attributes between those suppliers and the receiving organisation. Tightly controlled service-level contracts for high-risk deliverables are being supplemented by joint service agreements for medium-risk contracts with the free exchange of data and knowledge.

PROJECT DELIVERY CHAIN

Physical inventory – whether equipment or material – must be controlled in projects. Although this is an area of neglect in many undertakings, the good practice of operations in assets and stock management should be applied to projects. Project managers might have a nonchalant attitude towards inventories resulting in excess stocks. The deliveries from suppliers, whether material or equipment, must be received, inspected and properly stored before use. The same attention to records and the control of goods from external suppliers should also be applied to internal suppliers.

In a project supply chain, 'building and installation' is the building block that makes things physically happen. It is where plans are executed in sites and facilities to produce goods or services for customers. This stage is comparable to operations management in manufacturing industries. However most texts on project management give only scant coverage on the topic of supply chain management.

In the context of project management, the final handover and closure process determines the success and sustainability of project outcomes. The skill with which the closure is managed has a great deal to do with the quality of life after the project. A successful closure is the destination of the project supply chain. The closure stage of the project may have less impact on technical success or failure, but it has huge influence on the residual attitudes of the client and end users towards the project.

PROJECT INTEGRATION

Systems and procedures are essential components to integrate the building block configurations of the total supply chain. There are three major categories of systems and procedures:

- external regulatory and internal quality standards;

- financial and accounting procedures;

- information and communication technology.

The activities of a supply chain are affected by both national and international regulatory requirements on packaging, storage, pallets, vehicles, working hours, tariffs and many other issues. In addition an organisation maintains its own quality standards and service-level agreements with its suppliers and partners. The bodies of knowledge and project methodologies such as PMI's 'A Guide to the Project Management Body of Knowledge,' *PMBOK* (2009) and the UK Government's preferred approach, PRINCE2 (2009), are powerful guidelines to integrate the building blocks of project supply chain in order to successfully deliver a project.

Another important issue is improving the financial performance of the project. In response to pressures from stakeholders there is a risk of overemphasis on the short-term financial performance. Consequently this myopic approach results in over-investment in short-term fixers and under-investment in longer-term development plans. There is a need for a balanced approach.

The Internet, now taken for granted, has seen the use of technologies to create electronic communication networks within and between organisations and individuals. The implementation of ERP, websites, e-commerce, electronic data interchange and e-mail systems have transformed the process of the exchange of ideas and the sharing of data in 'real time'.

Regular reviews of project supply chain are comparable to Sales and Operations Planning (S&OP) in operations management. S&OP is a cross-functional management review process to integrate the activities of the total supply chain. Project review gatherings are held regularly and their frequency and participation depend on the type of meeting. Project team meetings by work packages or task groups are generally held every week and led by the team manager. Project progress groups (also known as 'gateway' review meetings) usually take place every month and are led by the project manager. Milestone review meetings are convened at predetermined dates and attended by the project board and project manager. In addition ad hoc review groups (for example, pre-audit, health safety and environment, and so on) are also scheduled with specific agenda.

Quality and performance management acts both as a driving force of improvement and a fact-based integrating agent to support the planning, operations and review processes. The foundation of performance management is rooted to quality management principles supported by key performance indicators of the Balanced Scorecard. Project quality is defined with three dimensions, such as design quality (specification), process quality (conformance) and organisation quality (sustainability). Perhaps the most important determinant of how we perceive sustainable quality is the functional and holistic role we fulfil within the establishment. It is only when a project organisation begins to change its approach to a holistic culture, emphasising a single set of numbers based on transparent measurement with senior management commitment, that the 'organisation quality' germinates.

Summary

In this chapter we have explained the characteristics and roles of supply chain building blocks in Total Supply Chain Management. The building blocks consist of nine components out of which six are for supply chain configuration (customer focus and stakeholders, resources and time management, procurement and supplier focus, supply management, building and installation and handover and closure) and three components are for supply chain integration (systems and procedures, quality management and regular reviews). These building blocks will be applicable, to a varying degree, to all types and strategies of supply chains regardless of whether they are in a major infrastructure project or a change management project or an information technology project. Supply chain management building blocks and integrating methods are key to ensuring that project materials and resources arrive as required, ensuring the success of a project.

13

Second Order Project Management
Making Sense of Complexity: Towards a Higher Order

Darren Dalcher

Is classical project management sufficient to operate in what is increasingly seen as a complex world?

The labels 'complex' and 'complexity' are increasingly being applied to describe the demands of projects and programmes. Indeed, the number and size of projects that merit the title 'complex' appear to be on the rise. Yet, practitioners and researchers alike identify the shortcomings of the traditional–classical approach of project management to address such features.

Delivering complex projects requires an understanding of complexity and uncertainty. Such projects are neither deterministic nor predictable and hence require a new toolset and a matching mindset capable of dealing with the challenges and uniqueness of complex situations. Traditional approaches to problem solving (thus including classical project management) rely on an essentially linear resolution process that reduces variety and relies on 'rational' decision making. By focusing on the execution part of projects, it becomes possible to zero in on short-term implications whilst ignoring the wider context of a project. The assumption of implied rationality also makes it possible to reduce the impact of having to deal with people with views, values and preferences. However the track record of successfully delivering complex projects by utilising methods that overemphasise efficiency and linearity is not good. Discounting people, complexity and context ensures that such solutions do not address the requirements and needs that made the project necessary in the first place.

The obvious conclusion is that current project management practice is not sufficient for successfully delivering complex projects and programmes. Complexity science and systems theory and science offer many new thinking tools and perspectives that are useful in re-framing and making sense of complexity, uncertainty and ambiguity. Project management practice now needs to expand and encompass such ideas and approaches in order to accommodate complex projects and situations.

The work of Michael Cavanagh is a good first step in that direction. Michael's book, *Second Order Project Management* is published by Gower in the Advances in Project Management book series.

Second Order Project Management combines approaches and perspectives offering rich insights for practitioners. The components include experiential learning, systems approach, appropriate contracting and outcome management. Many of the ideas also include fresh insights and new ways of addressing their impacts thereby offering a unique contribution to the discipline of project management.

While researching the book, Michael engaged in many conversations with leading practitioners who grapple with the complexity of projects. Conversations encapsulate fascinating insights and often reveal a deeper understanding of a context. Increasingly, researchers now turn to conversations to uncover deeper meaning and engage with a discipline and context in a new way. Michael recorded his conversations. In this chapter he attempts to share some of the voices and analyse the messages in terms of the implications to project management practice. His narration and commentary weave together a coherent discussion encapsulating insights, reflection and sense making.

While the quotes and interpretation are different in style and substance to the other chapters that appear in this book, Michael forces us to engage with the speakers and their message in a new way. The shared insights and perspectives are worth the 'pain' of having to think and see in a new way. Indeed, liked a skilled navigator, through his work and writing Michael offers us a way of overcoming many of the limitations of classical project management that form a requisite part of the next order of project management practice. The journey may uncover unusual ideas and require adjustments to some long-held perceptions and prejudices, but given our starting position, seems both necessary and exciting.

A Case for Second Order Project Management

Michael Cavanagh

Although project management has been around since a man built his first mud hut under the direction of his missus, it has only relatively recently become a recognised professional discipline, with formalised methods and tools being developed along the way. I can remember a time when just producing a Gantt chart would leave the client gaping with admiration; now we have some of the most sophisticated tools imaginable – Earned Value Management (EVM), PRINCE2, CMM-I and the rest. So why, it is reasonable to ask, do so many large projects still hit the buffers, under-deliver and/or blow their budget? Let me be clear – these tools and techniques (I'll term them 'first order') are absolutely vital; and up to a certain level of complexity, are quite good enough to do the job and deliver against a firm requirement. As the complexity increases, though, simply following the rules isn't enough – because in complex projects, the requirements aren't *ever* firm – in fact, the level of complexity is in direct proportion to their uncertainty. The project manager needs to be able to adapt, modify and improvise, applying first order tools to the specifics of the task at hand but in addition, deploying a range of additional, less prescriptive, techniques and methods as and when needed – and sometimes even 'breaking' the first order rules on purpose. These are 'second order' methods; and whereas first order tools are deployed to apply process rigour, the common element of second order approaches is that they are targeted solely towards the achievement of the deliverable purpose by whatever means. Put differently, first order is about doing things the right way; and second order is about delivering the right thing. It may very well be that the behaviours necessary to apply first order methods – attention to detail, rigorous adherence to process – could even be a barrier to second order management practice, in which creativity and lateral thought are the essential competencies, alongside systems thinking, experiential learning and courageous leadership.

During the writing of my book on second order project management, I was privileged to talk to some of the world's best and most experienced project leaders, whose track record demonstrates such abilities. One of the many qualities they showed in common was an enthusiasm to share their stories and their wisdom in order to inform the practice of others – a mark of true professionalism. Whilst I have attempted to incorporate their knowledge in the body of the book text, some of their most trenchant quotes deserve to be offered verbatim, in order to encourage careful reflection. For obvious reasons, they are unattributable.

'*Project management only becomes news when it's a bad news story.*' The 'hero' project managers – those who pull projects back from the brink of disaster – aren't really the ones at the top of their profession. The real heroes are those whose projects come in unspectacularly – on time, on budget, delivering the desired outcome. Their stories are rarely told.

'*People who come from well-organised, process-oriented backgrounds are not really able to understand complexity, and it's a mistake to push such people, talented as they may be, into situations demanding creativity and improvisation. It's the same in sport – Woods v. Ballesteros is a good example – and music – Clapton v. Hendrix. Talent plus lots of practice will bring great success, but never create genius.*' The normal route to leadership of complex projects is progressive, increased seniority relying on starting small and delivering gradually larger projects. The problem is that this tends to promote those who are accomplished first order practitioners, who may not possess the behavioural characteristics required for adhocratic leadership. It may be that first and second order project management should be seen as separate subdisciplines within the project management profession, and career development paths planned accordingly from an early stage.

'*OK, I agree that if it ain't broke, you don't fix it – but it **is** broke!*' The difficulty is getting people to *accept* that it's broke. Fear of blame, lack of mutual stakeholder trust, punitive contractual sanctions, and (perhaps most often) simple denial can lead to terminally-ill projects being kept on life support far beyond the point where recovery is possible.

'*If an organisation can't afford to get its budgets wrong, they need to accept the truth, however unacceptable. It is utter foolishness to believe that you can outsource risk.*' A way of dealing with the above is to pass the blame onto someone else. There is a tendency to feel secure behind rigorous contract conditions – '*if it goes belly-up we can always sue them afterwards*' but post-failure litigation can't deliver retrospective success.

'Even though we always get a lower performance than we expected, we are nonetheless incentivised to be optimistic.' An executive management mindset that is obsessed with setting ever-increasing stretch targets ignores the concept of elastic limit. A project manager who takes on something s/he knows to be unrealistic and probably unachievable deserves all they get.

'It is essential that we avoid the 'sunk cost' issues – past expenditure must never affect current decisions.' Peter Bernstein, in his excellent book *Against the Gods* (Bernstein 1996), makes clear the fact that human nature is not so much risk averse as *loss* averse. We would sooner throw good money after bad than write off what we've already spent. The English and French Governments' refusal to cancel Concorde even though it became clear that it could never become economically viable is a well-known example of this; it can also manifest itself when an expensive feasibility study finds that a project would be unviable – there is a feeling that the money spent would have been wasted if the project were aborted.

'Achieving greatness at anything equals love plus 10,000 hours effort.' Quoted often, this is not to be taken literally – what it means is that success is always a combination of motivation and effort. Even then, however, the effort has to be accurately applied. One of the most important principles I learned as a music student is relevant to experiential learning generally: *'Practice doesn't make perfect. Only perfect practice makes perfect'*.

'We adopted an approach euphemistically called "Preference Engineering" – doing things in the way people would like them done, when a business case could not be made for so doing.' This can be taken two ways. On the positive side, it allows tacit wisdom – instinct, intuition and inspiration – to override explicit knowledge. Conversely, it undermines the good governance practice of validating the Return on Investment equation. In the positivist business world, wisdom can often go unregarded in the face of raw data presented as inalienable fact.

'The West focuses on the short term; in the East the opposite is true. It's down to culture, and it's almost impossible to change overnight.' One of the most influential complexity drivers is project size – and the bigger the project, the longer its duration and the anticipated life of the product, with ramifications about long-term emergent issues. It is very difficult to reconcile adequate consideration of such issues in a promiscuous investment environment which looks for instant return.

'*Focus on outcome, and think about people.*' The trouble with people is that they are expensive, bloody-minded and, unfortunately, necessary. No matter how comprehensive the toolset, its effective use is subject to the vagaries of the human condition. The second order leader's prime task is to constantly ensure that the effort of the people-at-hand, with their skills and behavioural preferences, *in their current mood*, is applied as closely as possible to delivering the desired outcome. Abraham Maslow's hierarchy of human need (Maslow 1943) may be a simplistic model, but it's pretty useful as a start.

'*Human beings will always choose a route that best suits their personal experience, whether or not it best suits the task at hand.*' When addressing a new issue, we tend to operate through fixed mental models – looking for similarity to past experiences and sometimes shoehorning a 'fit' where one doesn't exist. What we're really doing is 'situating the appreciation' as opposed to 'appreciating the situation'. Again, leadership is needed here – leadership that is courageous enough to hear the opinion of others and accept that they might have a point, and disciplined enough to maintain a mind that is open to new things. '*The majority of our existing tools are based on what we see through the rear view mirror.*'

'*We still have the ability to build St. Paul's Cathedral – but we probably wouldn't.*' Of all of the interview quotes, this is the most enigmatic. In the course of discussing something else, I had asked a throwaway question whether we had forgotten some of the skills of the past – using the example of the Egyptian Pyramids – no one really knows how they were built. The answer was 'yes' – but *why* probably wouldn't we? Because our culture doesn't allow for non-functional, purely aesthetic additions? Because we'd never get planning permission? Because we have better ways of building? Because we'd never get the funding? The discussion moved on, I didn't pursue the point and haven't had opportunity to do so since. I wish I had.

'*"Lean" doesn't work with complex projects – you need resource redundancy.*' By definition, complex projects are unpredictable. If we know exactly what we have to do, and have the known capability to do it, we can plan to the last detail with a high degree of confidence in our estimates. 'Lean' is a great first order concept. It is potentially disastrous when we shall have to address unknown unknowns.

'*The system is designed to produce the outcomes we're getting. We consistently use the low bid price as the basis of the budget. When it all goes wrong, we should ask ourselves "What did you expect?"*' We won't, though. We shall look for other causes and explanations, and we shall do exactly the same next time. One of the visions of a good experiential learning programme is 'We will never make the same mistake twice'. This tends to attract two different responses. One of them is 'We shouldn't *make* mistakes at all!' This sort of comment merely reflects the stupidity of the speaker. The other – made by people who actually know what they're talking about – is 'We'd be happy if we could reduce the number of times we make the same mistake down to double figures'.

'In reality, Liquidated Damages drive bad behaviour – they are used as a financial recovery tool, but you'll have paid extra to get them. If contracts are punitive, they will result in a loss-loss situation – a combination of poor service to the customer and financial pain for the supplier.' Imagine a situation where significant daily Liquidated Damages (LDs) will be applied if you, as project manager, don't release the product to factory acceptance testing on a contractually-agreed date. You know of a slight enhancement which will take a couple of days to implement, but doing so would mean that you miss the date and the LDs would kick in. If, however, you release the product and implement the enhancement later, it will necessitate regression testing taking three or four weeks, but you could charge the customer for this. It is not operationally critical – it will simply result in slightly reduced performance under rare circumstances. The choice is yours.

'Our priorities are cost, schedule, resources – when really we should be thinking first about relationships, infrastructure and ways of working.' The latter are ways of delivering the former.

'Attempts to deal with complexity get strangled because the leadership hasn't the appetite for the fight – we get audited at a first order level, so that's what we make sure we do.' We often hear people say 'If you can't measure it, you can't manage it', or alternatively 'what gets measured gets done'. In practice, imposing rigorous measures results in behaviours based only on achieving those measures, whether or not they are appropriate. You'd better make damn sure you choose the right metrics, then. After all, Albert Einstein noted: 'Not everything that counts can be counted; and not everything that can be counted counts.'

References

Bernstein, Peter L. (1996). *Against the Gods*. New York: John Wiley and Sons.
Maslow, Abraham H. (1943). 'A Theory of Human Motivation,' *Psychological Review* 50(4):370–396.

14

Sustainability

Sustainability: A New Professional Responsibility?

Darren Dalcher

Who is responsible for sustainability?

Our last chapter focused on the growing complexity of projects, alongside the shortcomings of the classical approach to project management in dealing with an ever-widening spectrum of concerns. Projects increasingly involve larger groups and communities of stakeholders and hitherto uninvolved observers with more demanding interests, queries and issues. The current financial austerity climate makes it easier to shift our focus to short-term concerns, ignoring longer-term implications, yet, we are increasingly asked to apply extended life cycles, to consider decommissioning and safe disposal and to enable project artefacts to evolve and adapt so that they can be utilised in new contexts, situations or environments. Such thinking stands in stark contrast to the focus on short-term financial gains, as it implies an intelligent and meaningful long-term engagement with the future.

Earlier chapters homed in on professionalism and values as crucial aspects of developing a mature project management practice. We have also been exploring the need for richer insights for practitioners as they endeavour to operate in an increasingly complex and uncertain environment. Organisations operate in increasingly dynamic environments requiring holistic understanding of context, causal links and implications.

Indeed, once we acknowledge that projects enable organisations to adapt and achieve their objectives, it becomes easier to make tradeoffs, improve decision making and consider the longer-term implications of our actions. We recognise that focusing on technical or economic aspects is insufficient, as we need to consider the needs of different stakeholders and adopt a more social approach to analysing impacts and concerns. Moreover, we are increasingly concerned with the context of projects, and hence become more receptive to acknowledging the environmental milieu within which we operate and the relationships that it holds with other aspects. If project management is concerned with the delivery of the future, the decisions that we make now as part of our projects will play a key part in shaping that future.

The chapter by Gilbert Silvius and Ron Schipper encourages project managers to take responsibility for their actions and adopt a more holistic approach to projects and project management that embraces sustainability. The chapter offers a brief summary of some of the ideas and concepts that appear in the book *Sustainability in Projects and Project Management* authored by Gilbert Silvius, Ron Schipper, Julia Planko, Jasper van den Brink and Adri Köhler.

Sustainability can be addressed at many different levels. The authors make an important contribution in acknowledging that we can apply sustainable thinking and reasoning in project management processes, in project delivery, in project management, in the project and in the project life cycle. They argue that embracing sustainability, alongside complexity and uncertainty, is an inevitable part of the professionalism expected of project managers. As we manage and deliver change, we inevitably become responsible for the impacts and outcomes that it delivers. By adopting a longer-term perspective that encompasses sustainability we can enrich the dialogue around projects and utilise new ways of balancing economic, environmental and social concerns.

Sustainability is not simply about adopting a green approach. It is about accepting a greater responsibility as professionals. The methods, perspectives and new ways of sustainable thinking will enrich the repertoire of approaches available to project managers. While they carry the potential to maximise resources and get more out of limited budgets, they also enable us to consider implications from a wider perspective and perform better-informed tradeoffs. Their value therefore is in enabling us to balance more concerns; in offering more holistic perspectives, and perhaps above all, in coaxing us to assert our professionalism during project deliberations.

Taking Responsibility:
The Integration of Sustainability and Project Management

Gilbert Silvius and Ron Schipper

'The further development of the project management profession requires project managers to take responsibility for sustainability.' With this call-to-action, IPMA Vice-President Mary McKinlay opened the 2008 World Congress of the International Project Management Association (IPMA). Now, five years later, *Sustainability in Project Management*, elaborates on McKinlay's call and provides guidance on why project managers should take sustainability into account in their projects, how they can do this and on what steps to take. But isn't the sustainability of the project the responsibility of the project sponsor? And isn't the project manager bound by the scope, budget and time schedule of the project assignment? Authors Gilbert Silvius and Ron Schipper explain why project managers should take that responsibility.

Introduction

In the last 10 to 15 years, the concept of sustainability has grown in recognition and importance. The pressure on companies to broaden their reporting and accountability from economic performance for shareholders to sustainability performance for all stakeholders has increased. The recent world crises may even imply that a strategy focused solely on shareholder value is no longer viable. Following the success of Al Gore's 'inconvenient truth', awareness seems to be growing that a change of mindset is needed, both in consumer behaviour and in corporate policies. How can we develop prosperity without compromising the life of future generations? Proactively or reactively, companies are looking for ways to integrate the notion of sustainability in their marketing, corporate communications, annual reports and in their actions.

'In essence, sustainable development is a process of change.' This link between sustainability and change was already established by the UN World Commission on Development and Environment in 1987. And since projects can be considered as temporary organisations that deliver (any kind of) change to organisations, products, services, business processes, policies or assets, sustainability links to projects in the sense that sustainable development requires projects. In 2006, Association for Project Management President Tom Taylor recognised that 'project and programme managers are significantly placed to make contributions to sustainable management practices' and called upon the project management community to assume responsibility for a more sustainable development. However, Mohamed Eid concludes in his 2009 book *Sustainable Development and Project Management* that the standards for project management 'fail to seriously address the sustainability agenda'.

This chapter explores the concepts and principles of sustainability and their application and relevance to project management.

The Concepts of Sustainability

In 1972 the 'Club of Rome', an independent think tank, published its book *The Limits to Growth*. In the book, the authors concluded that if the world's population and economy continue to grow at their current speeds, our planet's natural resources would approach depletion. *The Limits to Growth* fuelled a public debate, leading to the installation of the Brundtland Commission. Their 1987 report 'Our Common Future' defines sustainable development as 'development that meets the needs of the present without compromising the ability of future generations to meet their own needs'. By stating that 'in its broadest sense, sustainable development strategy aims at promoting harmony among human beings and between humanity and nature', the report implies that sustainability requires also social and environmental perspectives, alongside the typically used economical perspective, on development and performance.

The vision that none of the development goals of economic growth, social well-being and a wise use of natural resources can be reached without considering and affecting the other two became widely accepted.

John Elkington developed this notion into the 'triple bottom line' or 'Triple-P (People, Planet, Profit)' concept: Sustainability is about the balance or harmony between economic sustainability, social sustainability and environmental sustainability.

But sustainability is a more holistic concept than balancing 'profit' with people and planet aspects. For example the new ISO 26000 guideline on social responsibility identifies 'transparency', 'accountability' and 'proactive stakeholder engagement' as some of the principles related to an organisation's responsibility to contribute to sustainable development.

Based on the concepts and standards of sustainability, a number of key elements, or principles, of sustainability can be derived. These principles of sustainability are:

SUSTAINABILITY IS ABOUT BALANCING OR HARMONISING THE SOCIAL, ENVIRONMENTAL AND ECONOMICAL INTERESTS

In order to contribute to sustainable development, a company should satisfy all 'three pillars' of sustainability: social, environmental and economic.

SUSTAINABILITY IS ABOUT BOTH SHORT-TERM AND LONG-TERM ORIENTATION

A sustainable company should consider long-term consequences of their actions, and not only focus on short-term gains.

SUSTAINABILITY IS ABOUT LOCAL AND GLOBAL ORIENTATION

The increasing globalisation of economies affect the geographical area that organisations influence. The behaviour and actions of organisations therefore have an effect on economical, social and environmental aspects, both locally and globally.

SUSTAINABILITY IS ABOUT CONSUMING INCOME, NOT CAPITAL

Sustainability implies that the natural capital remains intact. This means that the extraction of renewable resources should not exceed the rate at which they are renewed, and the absorptive capacity of the environment to assimilate waste, should not be exceeded.

SUSTAINABILITY IS ABOUT TRANSPARENCY AND ACCOUNTABILITY

The principle of transparency implies that an organisation is open about its policies, decisions and actions, including the environmental and social effects of those actions and policies, to stakeholders that could be interested in or affected by these actions. The principle of accountability implies that an organisation accepts responsibility for its policies, decisions and actions, and is willing to be held accountable for these.

SUSTAINABILITY IS ALSO ABOUT PERSONAL VALUES AND ETHICS

Sustainable development is inevitably a normative concept, reflecting values and ethical considerations of the society. Part of the change needed for a more sustainable development will therefore also be the implicit or explicit set of values that project management professionals, business leaders or consumers have and that influence or lead their behaviour.

These sustainability principles provide guidance for the analysis of the impact of the concepts of sustainability in projects and project management in the following section.

Sustainability in Projects and Project Management

Projects and sustainable development are probably not 'natural friends'. Table 14.1 illustrates some of the inherent differences in the characteristics of the two concepts.

Table 14.1   The contrast between the concepts of sustainable development and project management

Sustainable Development	Project Management
Long-term and short-term oriented	Short-term oriented
In the interest of this generation and future generations	In the interest of sponsor/stakeholders
Life cycle oriented	Deliverable/result oriented
People, Planet, Profit	Scope, time, budget
Increasing complexity	Reduced complexity

The relationship between sustainability and project management is still an emerging field of study (Gareis et al. 2009). Some initial studies and ideas have been published in recent years. And although the studies differ in approach and depth, the following 'areas of impact' can be concluded.

PROJECT CONTEXT

Project management processes should address questions such as: How do the principles and aspects of sustainability influence the societal and organisational context of the project? And: How is this influence relevant or translated to the project?

STAKEHOLDERS

The principles of sustainability, more specific the principles 'balancing or harmonising social, environmental and economic interests', 'both short term and long term' and 'both local and global', will likely increase the number of stakeholders of the project. Typical 'sustainability stakeholders' may be environmental protection pressure groups, human rights groups and non-governmental organisations.

PROJECT CONTENT

Integrating the principles of sustainability will influence the definition of the result, objective, conditions and success factors of the project, for example the inclusion of environmental or social aspects in the project's objective and intended result.

BUSINESS CASE

The influence of the principles of sustainability on the project content will also need to be reflected in the project justification. The business case of the project may need to be expanded to include non-financial factors that may refer to, for example, social or environmental aspects.

PROJECT SUCCESS

Related to the project justification in the business case, it should be expected that the principles of sustainability are also reflected in the definition or perception of success of the project.

MATERIALS AND PROCUREMENT

The processes concerned with materials and procurement provide a logical opportunity to integrate aspects of sustainability, for example non-bribery and ethical behaviour in the selection of suppliers.

PROJECT REPORTING

Since the project progress reports logically follow the definition of scope, objective, critical success factors, business case and so on from the project initiating and planning processes, the project reporting processes will be influenced by the inclusion of sustainability aspects.

RISK MANAGEMENT

With the inclusion of environmental and social aspects in the project's objective, scope and or conditions, logically also the assessment of potential risks will need to evolve to match the wider scope of interest.

PROJECT TEAM

Another area of impact of sustainability is the project organisation and management of the project team. Especially the social aspects of sustainability, such as equal opportunity and personal development, can be put to practice in the management of the project team.

ORGANISATIONAL LEARNING

A final area of impact of sustainability is the degree to which the organisation learns from the project. Sustainability also suggests minimising waste. Organisations should therefore learn from their projects in order to not 'waste' energy, resources and materials on their mistakes in projects.

These areas of impact provide ground for understanding the implications of integrating sustainability in projects and project management. These implications will first of all relate to the processes, methodologies and standards of project management. Secondly, these implications may affect the competences of the project manager. And thirdly, the implications may affect the way organisations plan and govern their projects.

   The obvious question that arises is 'What's new?' Well, the integration of sustainability requires various shifts in the way project managers see their profession: a 'scope shift' in the management of projects; from the classical constraints to managing social, environmental and economic impact. It requires a 'paradigm shift': from a predictability and controllability approach to an approach that acknowledges flexibility, complexity and opportunity. And finally a 'mind shift': the change where the project community realises that sustainability is no longer exclusively the responsibility of the project sponsor, but also the responsibility of the project manager with ethics and transparency as a basic touchstone. Such implications transform how projects are viewed, requiring everyone who is involved in the execution, commissioning, management or governance of projects to understand the new shifts that are taking place.

Conclusion

Organisations need to transform their operations, products and services in order to contribute to sustainable development. Projects are temporary organisations that deliver change to organisations. The project management community therefore needs to understand, accept and deliver their responsibility in realising sustainable development. Nowadays this is hardly a choice; it is an increasingly expected (professional) responsibility that the project management profession needs to urgently act upon!

References and Further Reading

Brundtland Report (1987). *Report of the World Commission on Environment and Development: Our Common Future*. Oxford: Oxford University Press.

Eid, Mohamed (2009). *Sustainable Development and Project Management*. Cologne: Lambert Academic Publishing.

Elkington, John (1997). *Cannibals with Forks: The Triple Bottom Line of the 21st Century Business*. Oxford: Capstone Publishing.

Gareis, Roland, Huemann, Martina and Martinuzzi, Andre (2009). *Relating Sustainable Development and Project Management*. Berlin: IRNOP IX.

15

Psychology
The Psychology of Projects: What the Bodies of Knowledge Don't Tell Us

Darren Dalcher

New project managers often enthuse about the methods, models, processes, charts, gates and procedures that enable projects to deliver. They are keen to jump straight in and apply the tools and methods to deliver the promised results. Such tools are certainly useful and essential but they are limited. Over the last few chapters we have considered issues to do with people, teams, resistance to change, politics, expectations, communication and leadership. Indeed, various surveys focused on project failures serve to remind us that our lack of understanding of the 'softer issues' is contributing to the failure of projects. Yet, the bodies of knowledge we utilise in project management are reasonably silent over such matters.

Decades of research into success factors, organisational maturity and process improvement have not delivered a clear recipe for implementing success in projects. Bodies of knowledge deliver procedures, tools and perspectives which consistently prove insufficient. Indeed, the key issue appears to revolve around meeting the people challenges in project management. Projects are done by people, for people. Project work is carried out in teams embedded within, and working for, organisations. The results of any project need to be acceptable to stakeholders, users, clients, and team members. Project leaders are expected to motivate teams, overcome resistance to change and communicate their vision. They also need to communicate progress, master organisational politics and motivate team members. Empowerment, communication, leadership, empathy, engagement, decision making and conflict resolution thus become the hallmarks of capable and competent leadership and management in the project delivery arena.

Where can we find out more about improving our softer skills, dealing with people, communicating effectively and handling risk and conflict? Psychologists have been involved in transforming the knowledge and skills related to organisational performance. Occupational and organisational psychology are concerned with how people perform at work and how to increase the effectiveness of people, teams and organisations. Their research is often focused on how teams form, behave and perform within organisations, whilst aiming to improve the job satisfaction and commitment of individuals. Moreover, in the last two decades an improved understanding of change management has yielded many crucial insights, contributing to the development of new models, tools and perspectives that are ready to be utilised by anyone interested in implementing change successfully.

The recent book *Project Psychology* by Sharon De Mascia, published by Gower, offers a glimpse into alternatives bodies of knowledge and expertise that can be of great use to project managers. Sharon is a chartered business psychologist with experience and interest in project work. She offers project managers a distilled compilation of ideas and approaches that can be utilised to improve project management practice in the areas that are not particularly well covered by the bodies of knowledge. The following chapter draws upon some of the ideas and perspectives that are explored in her book.

The human side of change continues to offer a major challenge to project managers. Sharon's contribution is in offering a new place to look for ideas. Our last chapter focused on the need to consider sustainability in project management. Project managers were encouraged to take long-term responsibility for their actions and adopt a more holistic approach to projects. It was argued that sustainability can be addressed at many different levels developing a richer understanding of projects. The legacy and success of projects will continue to be viewed as critical elements related to the change delivered by projects. Indeed, sustainability is borne out of the need to consider people and their relationship with the environment around them.

Project psychology facilitates an improved focus on creating sustainable change. Indeed, making change last, or stick, has been a major concern in the change management literature. By adopting a human-centric approach and considering a wider range of issues related to motivation, clarity of vision, communication, teamwork, reward, training and development, and leadership we can begin to address some of the concerns. Project psychology can offer us some of the tools we need to embark on that journey. Delivering without carrying the people with us is no longer possible. Opening up to new perspectives and considering the human contribution offers another part of the puzzle that we need to work through in order to create a more comprehensive tapestry of the knowledge, skills and perspectives needed to deliver successfully on a consistent basis. Learning to consider others and their needs is part of this journey towards greater professionalism and improved holistic understanding of our needs, the teams we form to get there, the organisations we work within and our connection to our wider context and environment.

The Psychology of Project Management

Sharon De Mascia

A very high percentage of projects are concerned with bringing about organisational change and yet project managers often fail to take sufficient account of the psychological processes involved in managing change and people. There has been a great deal of research carried out over the years, looking at why projects have such a high failure rate and various explanations have been suggested. Emerging research has indicated that the softer, people management skills are the ones that differentiate between success and failure, as opposed to the more technical skills. Much of the research and practice in organisational psychology can be applied to project management in order to maximise the chances of delivering a successful project.

Selecting the Best Project Team

The success of a project will depend on many factors, however, the efficacy of the project team and the project manager are important factors in the success of the project. Research has identified that there are certain skills and attitudes that are more likely to bring about success in a project team.

Project teams need to:

- have high levels of communication and influencing skills;

- be able to build sustainable relationships;

- be able to bond not only with the rest of the project team but also with people outside the team.

This means that project team members will need to have a certain level of 'emotional intelligence' (EQ). Emotional intelligence is a type of social intelligence that involves the ability to monitor one's own feelings and emotions and those of the people around us. Project team members also need to be able to operate with minimum supervision. This skill is more necessary in project teams because they tend to be more fluid, are often not co-located and can be very fast paced. The lack of close supervision also means that team members need to be more supportive of each other in order to ensure that the team operates as a coherent unit. They also need to be personally resilient and flexible.

How do you Select People with these Skills?

Project team members are often allocated to teams because they have the technical skills required, or sometimes just because they happen to be available at the time. This is not necessarily a good way to allocate people to project teams, particularly in the light of the skills and attitudes that we have mentioned above. The field of organisational psychology offers a range of tools and techniques to ensure that the best people are selected for project teams and there are a number of valid and reliable psychometric tests that can be used to select people with the key, skills and attitudes to deliver successful projects.

Leading the Project Team

Research into leadership has demonstrated that strong leadership is crucial to the success of projects. So, which is the best leadership style for a project manager to use in order to deliver successful projects? There are many different theories of leadership, however, given that projects are about change, the more visionary and engaging leadership styles are likely to be more successful, for example, Authentic Leadership, Emotionally Intelligent Leadership and Transformational Leadership. The project manager's ability to motivate and inspire the project team is a significant factor in project success. This means that project managers need to understand the different leadership styles and have the ability to flex their leadership style to match the maturity/requirements of individual team members and the particular situation.

Building the Project Team and Managing the Team Dynamics

Once the right people have been selected, it is important that the project manager creates the type of culture and team environment that is going to facilitate successful project delivery. Three factors have been found to be crucial in facilitating good team relationships, that is, integration, shared understanding and mutual trust. The project manager will need an understanding of the abilities and limits of each individual team member and must be prepared to invest in the development of project team members. Positive psychology emphasises the importance of our individual 'signature' strengths and project managers should allocate project tasks to team members on the basis of these strengths (and goal setting theory), in order to maximise team engagement and motivation.

Managing Team Dynamics

Over the years there has been a wealth of research into team processes and the factors that contribute to team cohesion. Project managers should have an understanding of team dynamics. They also need to have some awareness of each team member's preferred way of working in team situations and how each of the team members relate to each other and to people outside the team. It is important that team processes are monitored on an ongoing basis alongside task delivery in order to sustain team cohesion and high performance.

Managing Conflict

Project managers can often find themselves in a position where they are in conflict with one or more stakeholders. The traditional methods of addressing conflict by finding a 'middle ground' are not always in the best interests of the project as the 'middle ground' may compromise project objectives/delivery. Emerging research into emotional intelligence and positive psychology suggests that a more helpful approach might be to use conflict constructively to bring about a shared understanding and development for the project team. This can be achieved by using positive emotions to facilitate open discussion and by adopting a win/win mentality.

Engaging Stakeholders

Within the field of organisational psychology, there has been a tremendous amount of research into employee engagement and much of this work is applicable to the management of projects. Research has demonstrated that the key drivers for engagement are:

- a sense of feeling valued and involved;

- being involved in decision making;

- having the freedom to voice ideas;

- knowing that you will be listened to; and

- feeling enabled to perform well.

This suggests that project managers will need to take these factors into account in order to ensure that there is real, psychological buy-in from the stakeholders and that they are not just paying lip service to the project. This will ensure that stakeholders allocate sufficient time to the project and that they are involved in a way that is meaningful to them. This is more likely to create a sustainable bond between stakeholders and the project team.

Managing Risk

There have been many books written about the subject of risk in project management. Unfortunately, few, if any, of those books focus on the human aspect of risk and the fact that individuals are genetically predetermined to be either risk takers or risk avoiders. Project managers should be aware of individual team members' propensity for risk taking and there are psychometric tests that can be used to successfully measure this. There are also two other essential elements of human behaviour that need to be taken into account in association with any risk management process, that is, organisational factors (the wider cultural expectations and attitudes towards failure) and group factors (the team environment and group processes).

The People Side of Communication

Traditionally, communication within projects is planned in advance and the communication generally takes the form of highlight reports and various meetings. These methodologies are fine but they can have their limitations. Highlight reports can be good at conveying information but they are not very good at engaging and enthusing people. Meetings, on the other hand, do have this potential; depending on how they are managed. Project managers need to remember that communication is a human behaviour and is therefore affected by our cognitions, emotions and perceptions. There are various intrapersonal processes that project managers should be aware of, for example, perceptual distortions (generalising, 'horns and halo' effect, selective perception and so on) which all have an effect on the way in which individuals process information. More importantly perhaps, project managers need to have knowledge of interpersonal processes, for example non-verbal communication. When we communicate with others, around 65% of the information that people pay attention to is non-verbal. A knowledge of communication as a human behaviour coupled with a greater understanding of stakeholders and their preferences with regard to communication mediums will facilitate the sort of communication that motivates stakeholders and engages them in the project.

Change Management

The vast majority of projects bring about some form of organisational change; however, project plans tend to be about hard tasks which have to be delivered and often do not take account of the highly charged emotional atmosphere that change can engender. This means that you can have the best project plan in the world but if you fail to take account of the human side of change, it is unlikely that you will be successful in bringing about sustainable change. There has been a huge amount of research in organisational psychology about how to bring about sustained organisational change and this is all very useful and relevant to project management. It is important that project managers have an understanding of the underlying psychological processes that people undergo when they are faced with organisational change.

16

Benefits

Overstating the Benefits?

Darren Dalcher

Benefits have long been associated with the deployment of technology and the use of decision making. Traditional decision-making approaches are often focused on the measurement and consideration of the costs and the benefits connected with an undertaking and cost/benefit analysis has evolved as a process for evaluating the desirability of an option, technology or policy. Such calculations are based on the assignment of monetary values to the positive and negative aspects of a decision, or option, enabling a direct comparison.

In the last 20 years the project management literature has come to terms with the idea of benefits realisation through portfolios. The main idea is to ensure that the benefits used to justify an investment can be realised and managed so that the performance of the system or policy matches the promise, and hopefully that the expectations derived from the promise and the business case are fulfilled.

What Came First, the Project or the Benefits?

More recently the idea of benefits has been linked to individual projects and the satisfaction of stakeholder concerns. Moreover, the success of a project is increasingly linked to engagement, relationship management and expectation management pertaining to disparate stakeholder groups. In order to reach such communities and measure the success of change efforts the idea of managing and realising benefits has gained prominence and is increasingly addressed through established processes.

However, projects are not meant to uncover benefits unless they are exploratory initiatives or prototyping attempts concerned with testing the feasibility or value of a particular approach. Indeed, projects are created and executed in order to deliver lasting and meaningful benefits to the organisation.

Delivering Benefits

Benefits are typically identified during project portfolio management. Indeed, a major shift towards the adoption of portfolio management comes from the need to measure, deliver and appraise benefits in an organised fashion. They provide the reason for launching individual projects that deliver identified chunks of change, with their associated benefits, which can be addressed as projects.

Transforming Government and Public Services: Realising Benefits through Project Portfolio Management, by Stephen Jenner, published by Gower, explores project portfolio management as a way of improving delivery capability by focusing on improving business cases, focusing on value and benefits, incorporating stage gates and devises new ways of operating in complex, politicised and confusing environments.

The business cases for many change initiatives, including projects and programmes, appear to overestimate the benefits, whilst underestimating the costs. Upon delivery, such initiatives may be judged as failures. The following chapter by Stephen Jenner attempts to explain some of the failures through the lens of cognitive biases, which play a part in inflating the benefits associated with a programme, or project. Indeed he refers to the delusional optimism of overemphasising the potential benefits during forecasting.

The work in this chapter is derived from a new guide 'Managing Benefits' which Stephen is developing for the APM Group. It offers an important glimpse into the need to get a better handle on benefit forecasting.

Ultimately, the decisions we make at the portfolio level will depend on our ability to correctly identify the costs and benefits. While we continue to overestimate benefits (and underestimate costs), we are destined to continue making flawed decisions resulting in misallocated funds, missed opportunities and insufficient insights. To deliver successfully we need to address the tendency of overstating the benefits and develop a keener understanding of the tradeoffs, expectations and potential value of what we offer.

Benefits Realisation – Building on (un)Safe Foundations or Planning for Success?

Stephen Jenner

Research consistently finds that organisations struggle to demonstrate a return on their investments in change – for example, the Office of Government Commerce (OGC) report that, 'Deficiencies in benefits capture bedevils nearly 50% of government projects'.[1] The issue is not peculiar to the public sector – Nobel prize winner Daniel Kahneman notes that, 'Most large capital investments come in late and over budget, never living up to expectations. More than 70% of new manufacturing plants in North America, for example, close within their first decade of operation. Approximately three-quarters of mergers and acquisitions never pay-off … And efforts to enter new markets fare no better' (Lovallo and Kahenman 2003). Similarly, change management 'guru' John Kotter says, 'Up to 70% of change initiatives fail to deliver on the benefits that they set out to achieve.'[2]

Research also indicates that in many cases the causes of failure can be traced back to the business case, and in hindsight the problems are all too obvious. Why might this be? Psychologists and other researchers have identified a series of cognitive biases and organisational factors that adversely impact the production of accurate and reliable benefits forecasts and business cases. These cognitive biases are firstly examined, before we consider the organisational factors that can also work against accurate and reliable forecasting. We then review strategies and techniques that can be used to overcome both factors.

---

1   OGC (December 2003) *Gateway News*.
2   Quoted in http://www.apm.org.uk/sites/default/files/APM_BenefitsManagement.pdf.

Cognitive Biases Affecting Benefits Forecasting

Lovallo and Kahneman argue in the *Harvard Business Review* that forecasters suffer from 'Delusional optimism: we overemphasise projects' potential benefits and underestimate likely costs, spinning success scenarios while ignoring the possibility of mistakes' (Lovallo and Kahenman 2003). Table 16.1 identifies five of the main cognitive biases and how they can impact on benefits forecasting.

Table 16.1   Five of the main cognitive biases and their impact on benefits forecasting

Cognitive Bias	Impact on Benefits Forecasting
Expectation or confirmation bias	The tendency for forecasters to select evidence that confirms existing beliefs and assumptions, and discount or ignore evidence that conflicts with these beliefs.
The planning fallacy	The belief that, whilst being aware that many similar initiatives have failed to realise the forecast benefits in the past, this won't affect our current initiative. This bias is illustrated below by the results from a survey of Senior Responsible Owners (SROs).
The framing effect and loss aversion	The tendency to value losses avoided more than equivalent gains. Hastie and Dawes (2001) note that 'most empirical estimates conclude that losses are about twice as painful as gains are pleasurable'. Thus business cases that are framed in terms of what might go wrong if the initiative were not to proceed, appear more compelling than if the same initiative's business case is prepared on the basis of the positive outcomes obtained.
Anchoring and adjustment	In preparing forecasts we 'anchor' on, and give disproportionate weight to, the first estimate (no matter how reliable or relevant) and then make insufficient adjustment to reflect the specific circumstances. For example, Collins and Bicknell (1998) argue that 'not all computing projects fail – only most of them. Now and again serendipity sees a company or government department buying and implementing a system that does as much as half of what was originally intended.' 10% contingency is therefore unlikely to be sufficient.
Groupthink	The tendency to confuse knowledge with assumptions – and this tendency is reinforced when the majority of those involved share the same set of beliefs and values. Thus we become overly confident in our forecasts and ignore counter information.

Note that what makes such cognitive biases so powerful is that:

- Firstly, despite the evidence of past forecasting errors, we are often unaware of them. Research by Moorhouse[3] found: 'Only 10% of SROs feel business cases and benefits realisation are adequately understood on programmes across Government and industry, however over 60% feel the understanding on their own programmes is adequate' – an example of the planning fallacy in action.

- Secondly, many are linked and reinforcing.

- Thirdly, they affect experts as well as the general population.

- Fourthly, many probability estimates (which affect our assessments of risk and the likelihood of benefits realisation) appear counter-intuitive – for example, the odds that at least two people in a room of 24 people will share the same birthday are better than one in two, and the odds rise to over 90% when as few as 36 people are present.

But another explanation for estimation errors has also been proposed – and it is one where the cause lies less in the cognitive biases that affect us as individuals, and more in organisational factors that mitigate against accurate and reliable forecasting.

Organisational Pressures Affecting Benefits Forecasting

Professor Bent Flyvbjerg at Oxford University has undertaken extensive research of transportation infrastructure projects – research with a global reach. He concludes that forecasts are 'highly, systematically and significantly misleading (inflated). The result is large benefit shortfalls'. The cause is what he terms 'strategic misrepresentation' which is defined as 'the planned, systematic, deliberate misstatement of costs and benefits to get projects approved'. In short, 'that is lying' (Flyvbjerg et al. 2005). This is not restricted to transportation initiatives – comparative research finds the same issues apply to a wide range of initiatives: concert halls, museums, sports arena, convention centres, urban renewal, power plants, dams, IT systems, oil and gas exploration, aerospace projects, new product development and so on (Flyvbjerg 2006).

---

3   http://www.moorhouseconsulting.com/news-and-views/publications-and-articles/bench marking-sros-attitudes-the-quandary-of-the-sro.

Other academics have reached similar conclusions – for example, in Australia, Lin et al. (2005) report that 26.2% respondents to their survey admitted to regularly overstating benefits in order to get their business cases approved. Ward (2006) reports an even more depressing situation in Europe, with 38% of respondents in one survey undertaken by Cranfield University openly admitting to overstating benefits to get funding with the traditional investment appraisal process being, 'seen as a ritual that must be overcome before any project can begin' (Peppard et al. 2006).

The cause is, according to Professor Flyvbjerg, either because it's in the economic interests of those making the case, or because it is expected by the project sponsor in support of 'pet' projects. In short, benefits are used to help justify the investment in a preferred solution – and so the emphasis is on identifying benefits, not as a basis for managing their realisation, but in order to justify the costs required.

Why is all of this important? Some say so long as all business cases are based on inaccurate forecasts it doesn't matter. But it is important because, firstly if we don't know the benefits to be realised from our investments, we can't make best use of the funds at our disposal – the 'good' lose out to the 'bad' but well presented proposals. Secondly, it's taxpayers' and shareholders' money that we are investing, and it is therefore incumbent upon those making such investments that they are able to demonstrate effective stewardship of the funds entrusted to them and a commitment to realising *all* potential benefits. Lastly, if we don't know where the benefits are we cannot manage them – and so the benefits management regime is built on unstable foundations.

Whether the cause is cognitive bias or strategic misrepresentation (or indeed both in combination) the result is benefits forecasts that are unlikely to ever be realised in practice. So the relevant question is how can we address this and what techniques can be applied to ensure benefits forecasts are accurate and reliable, and so lay the basis for their actual realisation?

Solutions to More Reliable Benefits Forecasting

The first step is to be aware of the psychological and organisational traps that can compromise forecasting accuracy. The trouble is that even where we are aware of these issues, we can fall victim to them. Consequently more formalised strategies are also required. Fortunately there are a range of techniques available that can help promote more accurate and reliable benefits forecasts – ten examples are outlined below under three categories.

CATEGORY 1 ORGANISATIONAL AND CULTURAL FACTORS

1. **'Start with the end in mind' with benefits-led change initiatives,** that is, initiatives where the solution is designed to deliver the required benefits. Here there is less incentive to overstate benefits as they are the rationale for the investment rather than being used to justify a preferred solution.

2. **Stronger leadership.** The National Audit Office (NAO 2011) highlight the importance of senior management 'setting the tone by encouraging honesty in estimates, challenging optimism bias and assumptions and being willing to stop projects which no longer make sense'.

3. **Effective accountability** frameworks that hold people to account for results, by tracking performance through to benefits realisation – if forecasters know that robust post-implementation reviews will compare forecast with actual performance, then there is more of an incentive for them to ensure their forecasts are realistic.

4. Requiring benefits forecasts to be **validated prior to investment,** and wherever possible, 'booked' in budgets, business plans, performance targets and so on.

CATEGORY 2 CHALLENGE AND SCRUTINY

5. Deliberately seek **disconfirming evidence** and ensure all business cases include both the evidence for and against the case – with credible alternative options being included wherever possible.

6. Linked to the above – ensure forecasts are subject to robust and **independent challenge and scrutiny**. A diversity of perspectives is crucial to help overcome 'groupthink'. Internal audit and non-executive directors can play an important role here.

7. **Regular review** – ensure regular stage or phase gates are held at which the benefits case is subject to review and apply the technique

of staged release of funding – with continued investment subject to review of the investment rationale and re-commitment to the benefits case, so there are no 'orphan' projects.

CATEGORY 3   MORE RELIABLE FORECASTING METHODS

8. **Reference class forecasting** – where forecasts of an initiative's duration, costs and benefits are derived from what actually occurred in a reference class of similar projects. Taking such an 'outside view' (as opposed to the 'inside view' where forecasts are built up by considering the initiative in detail) has been found to produce more accurate forecasts, by avoiding both the cognitive biases and organisational pressures identified above.

9. **Stochastic rather than deterministic forecasts** – using probability-based rather than single point forecasts.

10. Apply **the Delphi technique** – Surowiecki (2004) has demonstrated that groups often make better estimates than individuals – the so-called 'wisdom of crowds' effect. The Delphi technique makes use of this by seeking consensus from a panel of experts over several rounds of questioning, with the results of the previous round being fed-back to the panel anonymously. In this way the members of the panel are able to revise their conclusions in the light of the views of others. But what is crucial is that the group making the forecasts are diverse and independent – as Surowiecki says, 'The best collective decisions are the product of disagreement and contest, not consensus and compromise.'

Where does this get us? Well adopting such strategies helps address the twin dangers of cognitive bias and strategic misrepresentation – and in doing so helps lay the foundations for more effective benefits realisation management based on the concept of 'planning for success'.

References

Collins, Tony and Bicknell, David (1998). *Crash – Learning From the World's Worst Computer Disasters*. London: Simon and Schuster.

Flyvbjerg, Bent (2006). 'From Nobel Prize to Project Management: Getting Risks Right.' *Project Management Journal*, 37(3) pp. 5–15.

Flyvbjerg, B., Mette, K. Skamris Holm, and Søren, L. Buhl (2005). 'How (In) accurate are Demand Forecasts in Public Works Projects.' *Journal of the American Planning Association* 71(2), pp. 131–146.

Hastie, Reid and Dawes, Robyn M. (2001). *Rational Choice in an Uncertain World*. Los Angeles: Sage Publications.

Lin, Chadraham, Pervan, Graham and McDermid, Donald (2005). 'IS/IT Investment Evaluation and Benefits Realization Issues in Australia.' *Journal of Research and Practice in Information Technology* 37(3), 235–251.

Lovallo, Dan and Kahenman, Daniel (2003). 'Delusions of Success, How Optimism Undermines Executives' Decisions.' *Harvard Business Review*, 81(7), 56–63.

NAO (2011). *Initiating Successful Projects*, London: National Audit Office.

Peppard, Joe, Ward, John and Daniel, Elizabeth (2006). 'Managing the Realization of Business Benefits from IT Investments.' *MIS Quarterly Executive* 6(1), pp. 1–11.

Surowiecki, James (2004). *The Wisdom of Crowds*. London: Abacus.

Ward, John (August 2006). *Delivering Value from Information Systems and Technology Investments: Learning from Success*. A report of the results of an international survey of Benefits Management Practices in 2006.

17

The Burden of Making Good Decisions

Darren Dalcher

Making good and informed decisions has featured in many of the chapters published in this collection. Indeed, decision making is increasingly recognised as a key competence that both defines and underpins many aspects of modern management and leadership. The process of decision making and its application thus appear to provide a common interest in many disciplines and domains of enquiry.

The extensive works of March and Simon acknowledge that the understanding of decision making was essential for deriving an appreciation of the behaviour of organisations. In that tradition, behavioural studies of organisations often embody a descriptive understanding of the processes and influences required to make sense of organisational behaviour patterns. Moreover, Simon has subsequently reasoned that decisions account for the majority of what executives do within organisations, thereby justifying an intense focus on the processes and dynamics surrounding the identification, elaboration, search and choice stages involved in decision making. Many researchers have concluded that management and leadership are fundamentally about making good decisions.

So What is a Decision?

Decisions imply choice from between a number of possible courses of action. They are action oriented as making a decision often necessitates some form of planning and committing to a strategy that involves action. The decision situation is bound by a set of constraints that are associated with the situation, and the resolution process may add to the set of constraints as particular action sequences are accepted, rejected, assumed, implied or committed to.

Many decisions occur in complex, dynamic, novel and uncertain situations. Context is crucial as judgement rests on the way the world is viewed, analysed and interpreted. Any perspective that is adopted is therefore selective and limited. The scarcity of information is also related to the speed needed to reach agreement and finalise the decision.

Stress in Projects

In temporary environments, decisions often have to be made in speedy fashion. The implication is: that decision makers do not have sufficient time to analyse and review all the options; that only partial information can be gathered; and, that part of the context will not be explicitly stated and understood. Human attention is sometimes described as a scarce commodity and management by exception requires the making of decisions when a mismatch is identified. Decision making under stress often provides a trigger for urgent decisions that need to be made.

The chapter by Kaye Remington considers the role of stress in making decisions. Kaye looks beyond the fixation with panic, identifying the potential role of stress in improving performance. Indeed, stress can play a part in the search for adaptation and in the building of added resilience, which can strengthen the performance and behaviour basis.

The chapter provides a new lens for considering the role of stress and the potential impacts on the project team. Given that stress is an increasingly common condition in project environments, the lessons for leaders, and indeed, the discussion on different styles and approaches offer new ways of thinking about and engaging with decision making under stress.

Further insights into complex projects, communication, governance, innovation and culture are available in Kaye's book: *Leading Complex Projects*, published by Gower in 2011. The book draws on original empirical research into the successful leadership of complex projects, which included in-depth interviews with 70 leaders involved in the successful delivery of complex projects, meticulous collection and analysis of existing sources and thoughtful synthesis of the insights into useful lessons.

Decision making under stress will continue to be a challenge in project environments. Leaders are expected to develop the requisite resilience and adaptability required to guide complex projects towards a successful conclusion. Reflective thinking and active engagement will pave the way to developing a new understanding, and a healthier appreciation, of the role of stress in decision making, and in turn will highlight the crucial impact of rapid and effective decision making in leading, directing and guiding complex projects.

Decision Making under Stress – Advice for Project Leaders

Kaye Remington

At some stage or another in their careers all project leaders are forced to make decisions under conditions of stress. Project management is time dependent. We are governed by schedules, milestones and deliverables. As projects become more complex, with increasing demands from stakeholders and changing markets and technology, we need to consider how effective we are when making decisions under stress.

Stress has an interesting effect on our ability to make good decisions. However stress is not necessarily all bad. The jury is out on exactly how stress affects our decision-making capability but research is starting to raise some really interesting questions, and there are even a few answers.

The idea that stress might have an effect on judgement has only recently been formally explored. It was formally raised during a Congressional hearing in 1988 that was investigating compensation for the victims of Iran Air Flight 655, which was shot down by the US Navy cruiser Vincennes over the Persian Gulf (Hammond 2000).

Performance and Stress

For over 100 years behavioural scientists have been interested in arousal (through stress). Many will be familiar with the so-called Yerkes–Dodson Principle (1908) which is often incorrectly represented as the simple U-shape published by Hebb in 1955 (Figure 17.1). It suggests that performance increases with arousal to a point of optimal stress and then performance declines.

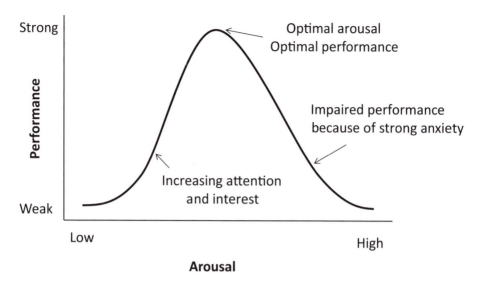

Figure 17.1   Hebb's version of the Yerkes–Dodson Principle

Hebb's (1955) version of the Yerkes-Dodson Principle – this version omits that observation that hyperarousal does not adversely impact simple tasks.

However this picture does not give the full story. It omits Yerkes and Dodson's observation that beyond this so-called point of optimum stress, increased stress can actually cause an increase in performance if the task is simple, reaching a plateau after which performance does not increase. It is only when tasks are difficult that performance declines with increased arousal due to stress (Figure 17.2).

Positive Stress is Good For Us to a Point

Positive stresses, such as the excitement caused by a thriller movie, a physical or mental challenge or an exciting football game are actually important for us to have in our lives. Without positive stress, we would become depressed and perhaps feel a lack of meaning in life. Not striving for goals, not overcoming challenges, not having a reason to wake up in the morning would be damaging to us. It keeps us healthy and happy. Eustress is a term coined by endocrinologist Hans Selye (1974) based on the work of Richard Lazarus (1966). Selye was one of the first stress researchers to acknowledge that stress is a necessity of life, stating that 'we must not – and indeed cannot – avoid stress' (1974:33).

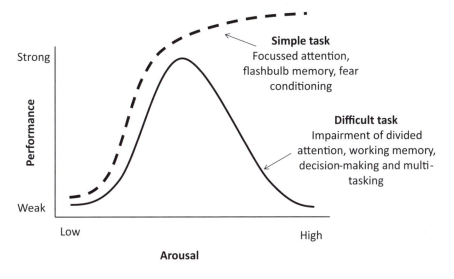

Figure 17.2 Original Yerkes–Dodson Principle

According to Selye the body has to mobilise biological resources to *adapt* or adjust to a stressor. Selye refers to each person as having 'adaptive energy'. This energy is finite however because the human response system grows exhausted and humans are born to die. In conjunction with this non-specific stress response are stressor-specific effects. For example, mental-frustration with a stressor can turn stress into distress, and may lead to undesirable physiological and psychological effects. Alternatively, demands that are challenging and lead to accomplishment or gain, and do not expend adaptive capacities, may turn stress into eustress, which is actually curative.

One much talked about subject associated with stress is the development of resilience, an essential characteristic for effective leaders. This chapter focuses on how we make decisions under conditions of stress. Leaders are primarily decision makers therefore it is about leadership performance under stress.

The Jury is Still Out on the Effect of Stress on Decision Making

Most researchers agree that not enough is known about how we make decisions while under extreme stress, the kind of stress that people experience when working with complex projects. It is often assumed that competence in judgement is always compromised under stress. For some individuals, heightened stress elevates their performance. Others are vulnerable to the negative impacts of stress, which results in diminished performance. For example an athlete knows that she or he should maintain a level of stress that is enough to stimulate top performance, but not enough to over-stress the body, because performance declines as the body becomes exhausted. This is an example of the Hebb's (1955) version of the Yerkes–Dodson Principle discussed earlier in this chapter.

A Qualitative Difference in How People Make Judgements Under Stress

Researchers have found a qualitative difference in how people make judgements under stress. Dorner and Pfeifer (1993) found that the problem-solving patterns were different for people under stress. These differences are important for leaders to understand when leading teams during periods of uncertainty that tend to occur in complex projects. We will return to their implications for project leadership later in the chapter.

- Stressed subjects tended to focus on the general outline of the problem, while non-stressed individuals relied on in-depth analysis.

- Consequently, stressed subjects made fewer errors in setting priorities whilst non-stressed subjects controlled their operations better.

Decision-making Patterns and Cooperation

There are other effects of stress that should place project leaders on their guard. Kontogiannis and Kossiavelou (1999) investigated the decision-making strategies and cooperation patterns of high performance teams under stress. They conclude that high levels of stress restricts cue sampling, decreases vigilance, reduces the capacity of working memory, causes premature closure in evaluating alternative options, and results in task shedding.

If, as seems to be the case based on research, leaders and teams tend to reduce the amount of information that they take in during periods of stress this is both an important and troubling finding. As a result of this behaviour, decisions made under stress are more likely to be based on impoverished information, at the very time when rich information is needed. Also, because stress has the effect of encouraging premature closure, that is people tend to make decisions before all the relevant facts are known, there is a high risk that the decision will be inadequate for the situation. As part of this process important tasks might be set aside without due consideration.

However, as we know, during conditions of uncertainty, when risks are rapidly escalating and key stakeholders are demanding a decision, an effective leader needs to makes a timely decision. In so doing he or she takes responsibility for the risk that the decision is the right one. Ultimately it is the leader or leadership team is responsible for the final call. Military history especially has demonstrated that very effective leaders tend to surround themselves with people and teams who will provide rich information and who are able to offer contrary opinions. Given the natural human tendency to restrict input during times of stress the challenge is to create a climate in which leaders and leadership teams have access to as much rich information as possible. In order to do this leaders must rely on their teams and in order to be able to rely on their teams during a crisis they have to know how to build and support their teams.

Building the Team to Support the Leaders during Stress

High performance teams during uncertainty and crisis:

- show high levels of flexibility;

- can perform tasks very rapidly;

- use implicit communication rather than explicit communication;

- use multidimensional information exchange rather than top down;

- anticipate the information needs of others and their leaders;

- comprise individuals who have achieved necessary levels of capability;

- have high levels of trust between each other and the leadership team.

A study of military commanders (Serfaty and Entin 1993) found that teams with records of superior performance have one common critical characteristic: they are extremely adaptive to varying demands. They also observed that the high performance teams in their study could maintain performance using just one-third of the time usually available to make decisions. However the mode of communication used by teams during stressful situations was different. Initially, the team responded to explicit requests in communications from commanders. As time pressure increased, they stopped waiting for explicit requests and instead provided commanders with information they implicitly determined would be useful.

These findings are consistent with what many of the senior leaders in our study reported (Remington 2010) and it is certainly consistent with what I have noticed in practice. Under conditions of uncertainty leaders must recognise that the normal top-down channels of communication are no longer the most efficient or the most effective. As one leader put it, 'In a complex project the leader can never know everything. The teams often know much more.' Acknowledging with the team that the leader cannot have all the answers opens the pathway to the kind of multidimensional interactive communication that produces a richness of information that the leader needs for decision making under stress.

These studies observed teams that were already performing at high levels when under stress. However they support the theory that if you want your team to be able to perform well under stress, team members need to behave intuitively with each other. Intuitive behaviour which manifests often as implicit communication does not happen overnight. It requires investment by leaders in the health of the team before the crisis occurs. It requires development of high levels of trust and respect for each other. They say that a team is only as good as its weakest link. Therefore leaders must seek to understand the composition and capabilities of their team members and make sure that any gaps in capability are filled well before any crisis occurs. The leaders in our study understood the value of taking time and effort to prepare the team for high performance so that when the inevitable crisis occurred they performed 'like a well-oiled machine'.

How Leaders Support Teams When under Conditions of Stress

Leaders can support their teams during periods of stress by explicitly:

- encouraging teams members to use their intuition;

- expecting team members to anticipate information needs of all stakeholders;

- within bounds of security encouraging rich and multidimensional information transfer;

- drafting high-level plans to allow for flexibility and rapidity of response by teams;

- protecting those assigned to detailed tasks from as much stress as possible;

- communicating trust in the team;

- avoiding micromanagement.

Communication is key to supporting teams under stress. Explicit communication applies to low workload conditions while implicit coordination needs to increase as the work load increases. Serfaty and Entin (1993) suggest that changes from explicit to implicit communication can help teams maintain performance under time pressure. Implicit coordination patterns, anticipatory behaviour and redirection of the team communication strategy are evident under conditions of increased time pressure. Leaders might encourage implicit communication patterns by updating team members frequently, encouraging team members to anticipate the needs of others by offering unrequested information, minimising interruptions to team members who are engaged with detailed or exacting tasks and articulating plans at a high level in order to allow flexibility in critical situations.

These findings have important implications for project leadership. If leaders are able to focus on priorities whilst protecting their teams from the full impact of the sources of the stress it is likely that the teams will be able to continue to perform operations effectively. However when leaders are stressed there is also evidence (Porter 1976) that they will revert to their preferred (most comfortable) behaviour pattern. This is one reason why we see leaders reverting to micromanagement during times of stress when they should be focusing on the big picture and leaving the details to their teams. Micromanagement usually serves to increase the stress for the teams rather than protect them from stress so that they can do the detailed operations and design work.

Conclusion

Although research into decision making under stress has a long way to go there is a great deal of useful information based on research which can help leaders and leadership teams build robust decision-making processes and avoid the many pitfalls that lead to poor decision making when under stress.

References

Dorner, Dietrich and Pfeifer, Erdmut (1993). 'Strategic Thinking and Stress.' *Ergonomics* 36(11):1345–1360.

Hammond, Kenneth R. (2000). *Judgments under Stress*. New York: Oxford University Press Inc.

Hebb, Donald Olding (1955). 'Drives and the CNS (Conceptual Nervous System).' *Psychological Review* 62:243–254.

Lazarus, Richard (1966). *Psychological Stress and the Coping Process*. London: McGraw Hill.

Remington, Kaye (2010). *Leading Complex Projects*. Farnham: Gower Publishing.

Serfaty, Daniel and Entin, Elliot E. (1993). Adaptation to stress in team decision making and coordination, Proceedings of the Human Factors and Ergonomics Society 37th Annual Meeting, Human Factors and Ergonomics Society, Santa Monica, CA., 2, 1228–1232.

Seyle, Hans (1974). *Stress without Distress*. NY: J.B. Lippincott Company.

Staal, Mark A. (2004). Stress, Cognition and Human Performance, Ames Research Center, Moffett Field, California, NASA/TM – 2004–212824.

Yerkes, Robert M. and Dodson, John D. (1908). 'The Relation of Strength of Stimulus to Rapidity of Habit-formation.' *Journal of Comparative Neurology and Psychology* 18:459–482.

Further Reading

Easterbrook, James A. (1959). 'The Effect of Emotion on Cue Utilization and the Organization of Behavior.' *Psychological Review* 66:187–201.

Evans, Gary W. and Cohen, Sheldon (1987). 'Environmental Stress.' In: Daniel Stokols and Irwin Altman (eds) *Handbook of Environmental Psychology*. New York: John Wiley and Sons, 1, Ch. 15, 571–610.

Gillis, John S. (1993). 'Effects of Life Stress and Dysphoria on Complex Judgments.' *Psychological Reports* 72(3c):1355–1363.

Hoffman, David A., Jacobs, Rick and Landy, Frank (1995). 'High Reliability Process Industries: Individual, Micro, and Macro Organizational Influences on Safety Performance.' *Journal of Safety Research* 26(3):131–149.

Hurrell, Joseph J., Jr. and Murphy, Lawrence R. (1998). 'Psychological Job Stress.' In: William N. Rom (ed.) *Environmental and Occupational Medicine*, 3rd edition. Philadelphia: Lippincott-Raven, Ch. 62, 905–914.

Kohn, Hugh (1954). 'Effects of Variations of Intensity of Experimentally Induced Stress Situations upon Certain Aspects of Perception and Performance.' *Journal of Genetic Psychology* 85(2):289–304.

Kontogiannis, Tom and Kossiavelou, Zoe (1999). 'Stress and Team Performance: Principles and Challenges for Intelligent Decision Aids.' *Safety Science* 33(3):103–128.

Kowalski-Trakofler, Kathleen M., Vaught, Charles and Scharf, Ted (2003). 'Judgment and Decision Making under Stress: An Overview for Emergency Managers.' *International Journal of Emergency Management* 1(3):278–289.

Lupien, Sonia J., Maheu, F., Tu, M., Fiocco, A. and Schramek, T.E. (2007). 'The Effects of Stress and Stress Hormones on Human Cognition: Implications for the Field of Brain and Cognition.' *Brain and Cognition* 65:209–237.

Pool, Robert (1997). *Beyond Engineering: How Society Shapes Technology*. New York: Oxford University Press.

18

Leadership Communication
The Art of Communication

Darren Dalcher

The recently released sixth edition of the *APM Body of Knowledge (APM BOK)* consists of four major sections: context, people, delivery and interfaces. While the management of typical project management 'things' such as scope, schedule, cost, resource, risk, integration and quality comes in the section focused on delivery, it is telling that the area concerned with people and interpersonal skills appears earlier in the table of contents.

Indeed, if we think about the typical shortfalls in terms of skills that impact many projects, and often lead to failure, the list may include diverse areas such as expectation management, trust, user acceptance, relationship management, stakeholder management, influencing, negotiation, conflict resolution, delegation and escalation. The common theme is the need to deal with people, and their needs, wants, expectations, preferences and ultimately their values.

Not surprisingly the first area featured in the *APM BOK* under the people area is that of communication. Communication is defined by the *APM BOK* as the means by which information or instructions are exchanged, which thereby provides the underpinning skill to address the shortfalls and overcome the barriers between groups and individuals in the project environment.

Whilst acknowledging that communication is fundamental to the project management environment, as poor communication will lead to misunderstood requirements, unclear goals, alienation of stakeholders, ineffective plans and many other factors leading to failure, the *BOK* proceeds to make a very powerful statement:

> *None of the tools and techniques described in this body of knowledge*
> *will work without effective communication*

Many qualifications and training courses focus on the knowledge, and increasingly, the skills and attributes required for effective project management. But the core skills of communication seem to have over-arching and underpinning value that connects and enables effective project management.

Yet, it is an often-neglected art. Unobscuring the path to wisdom and success is not explicitly addressed or acknowledged until we move beyond project management and delve into the armoury of the skills and capabilities underpinning project leadership.

Bennis and Nanus (2003) talked about the five leadership strategies, which include management of risk, management of attention, management of communication, management of trust and management of respect. Once again, one could argue that communication itself underpins the other four strategies and enables leaders to develop and share their vision, to delegate and involve followers and to develop the flexibility required to continue to learn and adapt.

Kotter asserted that management is a science; an active process, while leadership is an art; an interactive and inclusive engagement process. Indeed, focusing on communication makes project leadership much closer to the performing arts, where the leader utilises persuasive communication and power to induce audiences and participants to believe and share in the world, and the vision developed and enacted by the leader.

As we strive to interact with a growing complexity and uncertainty associated with our project endeavours, we are increasingly called upon to develop the leadership skills required to engage with stakeholders, risks, expectations and needs and to deliver meaningful change.

Advising Upwards

To facilitate successful projects, communication needs to occur in many directions. Upwards, downwards, sideways and all around. After all leadership often implies making things happen when we are not managing or when we are not in control. The chapter by Dr Lynda Bourne calls attention to the need to communicate upwards for effect. Communication upwards is concerned with conveying meaningful and useful information that is fit for purpose; in this case providing the required insights needed to support projects.

The following chapter explores the difficulties in using language as a means of communication, the impact of being overly precise, and the risk associated with fostering a false sense of precision and knowledge. It relies on the author's extensive experience in identifying and highlighting the issues associated with leadership, and stakeholder management and engagement. The chapter follows Lynda's recently published book, *Advising Upwards: A Framework for Understanding and Engaging Senior Management Stakeholders*, released by Gower. The book brings together a number of international experts offering insights into the decisions, risks and challenges associated with managing up.

Lynda's work has expanded the available knowledge regarding the management of stakeholders, and the recent chapter is a welcome addition to the literature on dealing with senior managers and sponsors and the impact of communication in such a context.

Progress requires leaders and managers to look beyond the tenets of management and to engage with the skills and capabilities associated with leadership. Unobscuring the path to wisdom and offering a true measure of progress relies on the gentle art of communication. Leadership entails developing the skills required to encourage the correct expectations and insights needed to facilitate effective support. Improving the less talked about aspects of managing project, requires embracing the core importance of communication and applying upwards, as well as downwards and sideways.

F. Scott Fitzgerald noted that genius is the ability to put into effect what is on your mind. To embrace successful delivery, practitioners need to ensure that the artful skills of effective communication are developed, fine tuned and improved continuously, thereby enabling all the other tools and techniques to work.

References

Bennis, Warren G., and Nanus, Burt (2003). *Leaders: Strategies for Taking Charge.* New York: HarperCollins.

Kotter, John (1990). *Force for Change: How Leadership Differs from Management.* New York: The Free Press.

Communicating Upwards for Effect

Lynda Bourne

Effective communication between project stakeholders is always difficult and misunderstanding and confusion are easily created. The key to effective communication is clarity created through simplicity. As Albert Einstein once said, 'If you can't explain it simply, you don't understand it well enough.' This is particularly true when trying to communicate project objectives to senior executives.

The communication problem is compounded by project management jargon, technical industry jargon and language differences. Within the 'project community' we have a range of terms that have a specific meaning, 'critical activity', 'time now', 'EV', and so on. People in the general business community frequently use the same words in similar context but apply completely different meanings. We say something; they attribute their different meaning and know they have understood exactly what we've said – but their understanding is not what we meant!

Albert Einstein also summarised the problem nicely: 'The major problem in communication is the illusion that it has occurred.' Without an accurate understanding it is impossible to agree, disagree or resolve anything.

Lewis Carroll considered communication in *Through the Looking-Glass, and What Alice Found There* (1872): 'When I use a word,' Humpty Dumpty said in rather a scornful tone, 'it means just what I choose it to mean – nothing more and nothing less.' Interestingly, Humpty Dumpty's view of communication is similar to that of most people's.

The trouble is if you want to communicate with a purpose, the listener needs to understand what you have chosen the word to mean and this is not helped by the English language! A few examples to confuse anyone:

- The bandage was *wound* around the *wound*.

- The farm was used to *produce produce*.

- The dump was so full that it had to *refuse* more *refuse*.

- We must *polish* the *Polish* furniture.

- I did not *object* to the *object*.

- The insurance was *invalid* for the *invalid*.

- They were too *close* to the door to *close* it.

- The *wind* was too strong to *wind* in the sail.

- After a *number* of injections my jaw got *number*.

No wonder the English language is hard to learn!

Whilst any language is superficially made up of words and words have meaning, context is critical. An example is, 'Since there is no time like the present, he thought it was time to present the present.' This sentence could be rewritten, 'Since there is no time like the present, he thought it was time to bestow the gift.' What's really interesting though is most people with a good command of English within the context of the whole sentence would have little difficulty in distinguishing between:

- present = the current time

- present = bestow or give

- present = gift.

But it's not that simple! Context depends on a whole range of factors including professional background. Ask an architect for the plans for a project and expect to see a bundle of drawings. Ask the same question of a Project Management Professional (PMP)-qualified project manager and expect to see a bundle of documents including the schedule, budget and scope. Same word different meaning based on the context the listener is working within. Your boss's context is almost certainly not yours and you need time and a two-way dialogue to ensure correct understanding.

No Understanding Means No Communication, or Worse, Miscommunication!

This is critically important because one of the keys to project success is managing stakeholder expectations; and the only medium we have to influence expectations is effective communication. But when communicating with senior stakeholders, their expectations will be based on what they understood we said, which as we have already demonstrated, may not be what we meant!

This is a major risk, particularly if the misunderstanding by senior stakeholders leads to unrealistic expectations that are unlikely to be fulfilled! Great care needs to be taken to avoid providing information in a form that creates impossible or inaccurate expectations.

For example, as project management professionals, we all know that our carefully prepared estimates of future cost and time outcomes are approximately correct, and the inevitable small estimating errors will lead to a range of probable outcomes, but we cannot assume our bosses have the same understanding. Despite knowing this, far too many project managers seem willing to create schedules that state explicitly that a task will complete at 3:30pm on a Tuesday afternoon in four months' time or the total cost of their project will be $10,988,547.55. These pseudo accurate estimates based on detailed calculations made by sophisticated software are no more valid than estimates presented in more general terms but the pseudo accuracy can easily create false expectations.

The figure of $10,988,547.55 is no more valid than an estimate stated in more realistic terms such as: $11 million with a probable range of -5% to +10%. Achieving a detailed estimate for an $11 million project to within a range of -5% to +10% indicates a very careful estimating process in a stable, well-understood environment; you know you have done a good job, but does your boss? The difference is the precisely wrong number calculated to the nearest cent will raise the expectations of a range of senior stakeholders as to degree of accuracy that can be achieved in an estimate, leading to 'perceived failure' when the stakeholder's unrealistic expectations are not realised. If your estimate is $10,988,547.55, it only takes a cost increase of $2,000 (an estimating error of 0.02%) for your project to 'fail' because the costs have 'blown out' from $10+ million to over $11 million.

Effectively communicating upwards requires the project team to look at the data generated by their spreadsheets and scheduling tools and then apply common sense to the way the information is formatted before forwarding it to senior stakeholders.

For effective communication, unnecessary detail, pseudo accuracy, jargon and ambiguous words should be removed and replaced with useful information framed in simple, accurate and realistic terms. There is a significant difference between simplistic and elegant simplicity; skilled communicators aim for easily understandable elegance.

From this base communication theory requires feedback and testing for understanding; wherever possible closing the feedback loop is the key to effective communication but this is not always possible. Recognising breakdowns in understanding in face-to-face conversation is fairly easy; but a confused look cannot be seen through the medium of an e-mail or when your boss is reading your report on her way home. It is only by thinking carefully about how you structure the information contained in your communications that you can increase the likelihood of creating clear understanding and reasonable expectations.

If this all seems like hard work, remember that unrealistic expectations are unlikely to be fulfilled, and if the unrealistic expectations are held by your CEO and your project fails to live up to them, you are the person who gets fired!

19

Sustainable Impacts
Sustainability and Success

Darren Dalcher

Many articles and conference presentations touch on the notion of project failure, promising to improve on past statistics. Indeed, we are developing a growing understanding of the core causes that underpin failure; but is this growing understanding both necessary and sufficient to deliver success?

Part of the answer depends on when we measure success. Success is clearly a relative term that is context- and viewpoint-dependent. It is also time-dependent as the view of a success, or failure, of a system or artefact may vary with time.

But there is also an essential contradiction. Projects are designed to deliver a product, or artefact as an end point. Delivery and handover can thus be viewed as a successful result of a project. Yet, this may lead to deeper questions about the nature of project management. Is project management simply concerned with the creation of something that did not previously exist, or does it go deeper and look at the need to make a difference, achieve an outcome, or deliver promised benefits?

If we accept the former, we have a project management that is focused on delivery. If we delve into the latter we are obliged to adopt a longer-term position, one that extends beyond delivery of a project into the benefit realisation and investment cycles.

Society has also become increasingly engaged with the concept of sustainability as it becomes increasingly obvious that the competitive race to accumulate profits has depleted resources and challenged environments.

The short-term focus of projects, which encourages immediate exploitation to deliver identified targets, thus stands in direct contradiction to the need to adopt a responsible stance and consider the impact on future generations. Indeed, we might even contend that projects, with their inherent race towards success, contradict the notion of sustainability. As we engage in more and more projects, we may forget to take a strategic view or ignore the long-term perspective. The more rapid the results, and the smaller the cycle of delivery, the less time we have for developing holistic thinking patterns and considering the longer-term impact of our decisions and actions.

Adopting sustainability as a core value and a strategic vision forces us to rethink our relationship with projects and change. It may also engender new thinking about growth, profits, consumption and their longer-term impacts.

Brulin and Svensson contend that even successful projects are viewed in a short-sighted way. Their research suggests that very few projects evaluate the long-term impacts. Moreover, it identifies an extraordinary level of failure in the durability of large change programmes and projects.

The following chapter is based on their book *Managing Sustainable Development Programmes: A Learning Approach to Change*, published by Gower. The book offers insights into the key issues required for long-term management with a sustainable focus. It provides practitioners with a new way of thinking and considering the role of projects and the benefits that can be delivered.

One of the key messages is the need to move from project management to project organisation. Project organisations are capable of fostering a longer-term perspective with an increasing focus on active ownership, collaboration and developmental learning. The key hypothesis of the work is that project organisation is fundamental to sustainable development work. The evidence amassed by the authors shows that active ownership and collaboration between different stakeholders and actors, combined with dynamics of developmental learning underpin such progress. Indeed developmental logic offers a new paradigm that extends beyond the familiar production logic.

The search for environmental solutions requires the questioning of existing paradigms. It also requires new ways of engaging multi groups of stakeholders and the development of proactive strategic thinking about our context, environment and the long-term implications of actions. By adopting a better-informed position we may begin our journey to play a part in shaping and sustaining our environment. Willingness to give up the urge to control combined with insightful and reflective practice can thus develop into new ways of making a difference.

Robert Gutman observed that 'every profession bears the responsibility to understand the circumstances that enable its existence', Our responsibility now is to invoke the long-term perspective when considering deliverables, benefits and investments, and the strategic and systemic aspects when addressing impacts and concerns to enable us to engage with change in new ways and improve our long-term track record for success. In considering the success of initiatives we are thus condemned to take longer before we form our judgements and pronouncements.

Sustainable Change in Large Projects

Göran Brulin and Lennart Svensson

Our research deals with how sustainable impact can be achieved from large projects and programmes. Sustainability means outcomes in terms of long-term effects from a programme – that is a cluster of projects. Our review of earlier programme and project initiatives indicates that sustainability has often been poor. Uncertainty about what projects lead to in the long term is great, since there is little research in the area, and few evaluations study long-term effects. Which are the mechanisms for successful sustainable development programmes and projects? What driving forces enable project results to continue, be integrated with regular operations, and disseminated to other areas and leading to strategic impact? There seem to be three mechanisms that are decisive:

Active ownership within the framework of an efficient and transparent project organisation.

Collaboration between important actors and organisations building on joint knowledge formation blended with action.

Developmental learning that leads to multiplier effects.

Learning through ongoing evaluation and interactive research in the Swedish EU Regional and Social Funds programmes shows that these mechanisms are the starting point for sustainable long-term effects. Hitherto, it has been difficult to draw overall conclusions from the ambitious programmes carried out to support regional growth, innovation and job creation. However, now it can be shown that lack of active ownership is evident in many projects.

This is a consequence of how projects are initiated, prioritised and steered. Projects are often initiated externally, from an intermediate level in the organisation or from the staff, which means that top management and line managers are not involved in taking long-term responsibility for initiated projects. It has also proved to be difficult to bring about learning collaboration between important actors and organisations, especially in large and complex projects that have been dominant during the current programming period. Innovation systems and Triple Helix also cover different actors with different traditions and cultures. The possibility of creating developmental learning leading to multiplier effects is limited by rules, routines and obstacles between projects, programmes and the system level.

There has always been the dream of total control and steering of programmes and projects. Intensified control, follow up and steering are however not the path forward. Rather learning systems should ensure that experiences and knowledge are condensed, packaged and transferred to the programme implementing authority, decision-making partnerships, local and regional development actors, partnering organisations, participating companies and others.

The alternative to the planning steered evaluation models is the development supportive evaluation model. Instead of checking that development initiatives and projects really implement activities and follow the plan for achieving measurable and controllable goals (in accordance with Specific, Measurable, Assignable, Realistic, Time-related (SMART) criteria), it involves learning through ongoing evaluation in order to provide support for development. The idea is that, feedback and generated knowledge accumulate gradually, and in the process shape the implementation, allowing it to move towards the general objectives. It is through continuous evaluation and learning that the different professions managing development processes – such as organisational consultants, venture capitalists, therapists and others – work. Putting together and combining insights and knowledge from a number of different organisations, companies and individuals in a similar development phase creates energy in programme and project implementation.

There are good examples of learning through ongoing evaluation, as well as interactive and action research, which have provided development support and thus played a strategic role for sustainable impact of programmes and projects. In this context it is important to consider profiles, competence and support from ongoing evaluators and interactive researchers. One observation is that management consultants playing this role only have temporary responsibility. If the person is a qualified 'researcher', he/she possesses knowledge about the ethical conditions and critical role of research. Learning through ongoing evaluation can also be developed through clearer competence requirements from financiers and purchasers. It is important to reflect on how knowledge can be built up regionally through such efforts and how they may contribute to affect systems and increase renewal in the long term.

Rather than trying to impose 'higher-quality, better functioning monitoring and evaluation systems', it is probably time to change the strategy on how to carry out large programmes. It is time to accept that they cannot be primarily monitored from above. A truly results-oriented approach is not about fine-tuning monitoring through remote control. On the contrary a results-oriented approach has to be based on an iterative learning system. The main task is, for example, for the commission carrying out structural fund programmes to knit together member states, programme managers and project leaders in more horizontal learning structures. The implementation of large programmes would then be based on joint knowledge formation in a global context, and also be based on theory and practice, as well as being transparent. Such an epistemology would transform programmes in the structural funds into a mechanism for knowledge-based development processes that support sharing of innovative practices regarding growth and job creation. In this way Europe could take decisive steps towards becoming 'the world's most competitive region'.

It is time to establish a fifth generation evaluation. Feedback from evaluation should be directed to a broader group – to participants, users/customers, financiers, industry, managing authorities and other target groups, both during the implementation phase and on completion of the project. Seminars, conferences and other meetings with different actors can be identified as important for dissemination and strategic impact. Learning concerning regional growth and development processes involves finding ways of concretely looking at similarities and differences through different themes and questions, lessons to be learnt and successful examples, as well as finding forms that actively involve different actors (nationally and regionally). Learning can take place through different forms for the exchange of experiences, and also in networks through bench learning. Each region is unique and must find its way of developing. Learning does not deal with copying what a specific region has already done, but rather providing opportunities for reflection to draw lessons from the experiences gained by others. It should be emphasised that sustainability is connected with the ability to resolve dilemmas and contradictions in a reflective way – and not just to look for simple solutions. Not least the experience of the worst financial and economic crisis to hit the world since the 1930s demonstrates the necessity of developing flexible and reflective implementation in programme initiatives. We summarise our conclusions in a number of recommendations and thought provoking questions:

- Make a careful selection of applicants to determine if there are conditions for active ownership. Is the motive to develop operations, obtain funding, or just to demonstrate participation in a project? To what extent have project owners been actively involved in driving and developing projects over the long term? Does good collaboration exist with other actors?

- What does the project organisation look like? Will there be a steering group that is competent, has a mandate and the capacity to work strategically, and steer in the direction of long-term effects? What different and complementary competencies exist in the steering group? Has a gender and integration perspective been used to create dynamics in learning processes?

- Are there conditions for learning collaboration between important and relevant actors and organisations? Do applicants understand the need to build relationships of trust and confidence, and do they have the capacity for mobilising and acting innovatively?

- Are there conditions for developmental learning that can lead to multiplier effects? How should interaction between actors at the local, regional and national level work in practice? Are there ideas on using intermediaries – such as higher education, research and development centres, industrial development centres, learning centres and others – for dissemination and strategic impact?

Practical advice and recommendations may be good, particularly if they have a theoretical and empirical foundation that can provide a stronger foundation, transparency and function strategically. The recommendations are not intended to function as a checklist nor a template for sustainable development work. Instead they should be regarded as a basis for a dialogue between applicants, project case handlers and decision makers on the rationale of a project, and above all how it can be made better. A dialogue-based learning process of this kind can preempt problems and enhance the ideas underlying the project. This involves, *inter alia*, the difficulties of managing programmes of this scope in a world where change has been made and continues to take place at a rapid rate over a short period of time in the economy and society.

The strategies for discoveries and innovation are often organised through top-down planning systems. The literature on project management is often based on these scientific assumptions with a focus on linearity, planning, regularity, measurement and confirmation of facts. By using this verification paradigm, the project managers will not find 'the black swans', namely rare and unforeseen events. Most projects are based on production logic, not on developmental logic. Such a linear change paradigm can function in a predictable, controlled and stable environment, but not in an open and rapidly changing society. In a complex and unpredictable world with extreme events, the models for calculation and planning are less useful. An alternative change strategy would be based on recognising opportunities in situations that are recognised as being complicated, fuzzy, rare, inconsistent, random, unknown, improbable, non-linear and uncertain. The discovery of the computer, the Internet and the laser have all been unplanned, unpredicted and have remained unappreciated well after their initial use.

20

Knowledge

Is There a Universal Theory of Project Management?

Darren Dalcher

Teaching project management is a challenge. First, there is the question of where to position the faculty. Should it sit within engineering? Or might it fit better in a business school? Or perhaps it needs to be positioned as a generic discipline, which applies in all domains and endeavours. Then, there is the question related to the philosophical underpinning: namely, is project management a science or an art? The award students obtain should reflect that orientation in its title. Once these aspects are out of the way, all that is needed is the body of knowledge (and the evidence that supports it).

Now, it might be tempting to settle for a set of processes and procedures as they help us to perform tasks more skilfully. Reducing skills into a set of procedures is appealing from a pedagogic perspective as it offers a natural structure that can be translated into a lesson plan and ultimately pared down to a set of steps to be memorised.

However, in reality we all know that the craft and discipline of project management cannot be reduced to chunks of knowledge. The skills, behaviours and interactions of successful project managers rely on understanding the complex interplay between people, organisations and change. Lessons from project failures have taught us to take heed of relationships, expectations, trust, communication, politics, conflict and even human follies and imperfections. Yet these aspects are not included in the formally published bodies of knowledge.

Practitioners increasingly talk about a mismatch between project management theory and practice. Some papers published in the academic literature even contend that project management theory is harmful to project management practice. In an ideal world the two would be intertwined so that practice is the source of theory, and theory leads to improved practice. Drawing on experience could thus become the source for generating the new knowledge required to make sense of the experiences and find their meaning. Continuing to explore and discover enables one to make sense of the environment and begin to address the challenge of uncertainty.

The question is what knowledge can we draw upon? The author of this chapter is offering to take us on a daring journey. Michael Hatfield, author of *Game Theory in Management*, recently published by Gower, is well known to many project managers for his insightful perspective on the discipline. In his chapter he challenges us to rethink the received knowledge and evaluate its effectiveness.

Bodies of knowledge have been with us for a considerable amount of time, yet as a profession we are still struggling to get organisations to adopt them. In a Darwinian economy those who do not adopt the received wisdom would be wiped out, unless that is, that wisdom was not a sufficient condition for success. Michael Hatfield is challenging the discipline to question the track record of the approaches.

The book makes a strong case for developing models to test the feasibility and usefulness of management decisions and their consequences. The book shows that the results of such modelling may question many of the underpinning wisdoms of management theory. Indeed, according to the findings, some of the management approaches advocated as best practice may prove to be detrimental in many areas of management. In the book and this chapter Michael is asking some very important and very uncomfortable questions. Indeed, what would happen if our bodies of knowledge were misconceived and counter-productive?

Arthur Conan Doyle observed that it was a 'capital mistake to theorise before one has data' as insensibly one would begin to twist facts to suit theories, instead of theories to suit facts.

A maturing profession should be questioning its basis of knowledge and evidence. The philosopher Karl Popper noted that whenever a theory appears to be the only possible one, it is a sign that we have neither understood the theory nor the problem which it was intended to solve. Over many generations, science has shown to be prepared to abandon an idea for a better one. Perhaps the test of where project management should be sited could depend on whether it has developed a similar way of adjusting to what may become a long search for universal understanding that will give us the undisputed theory of project management.

The Coming Sea-Change
in Project Management Science

Michael Hatfield

When Thomas Kuhn published *The Structure of Scientific Revolutions* (University of Chicago Press, 1962), he introduced into the popular lexicon the term 'paradigm shift'. Its original meaning dealt with the gradual shift in the adoption of a given, newly-introduced theory as it displaces commonly-held ideas that fail to adequately explain observed data or phenomena. In the realms of the hard sciences this idea displacement is easily observed and documented, as competing theories can be empirically tested for their validity. This is not so in the so-called management sciences, since the number of parameters involved in testing any theoretical approach within a macroeconomic environment is prohibitively expansive – it's simply impossible to isolate the contributing elements affecting macroeconomic transactions to the extent necessary to validate a given approach.

Within this environment, almost any reasonable-sounding hypothesis, backed by data that wouldn't survive scrutiny based on the rules of evidence, can be proffered and furthered well beyond its capacity to explain why things managerial have happened the way they happened, much less provide insights on how future events are likely to unfold. This does not stop bloggers, writers, institute founders, college professors and many others from attempting to introduce into the zeitgeist notions, structures, ideas and theories of how management ought to function, many of them suspect at best, fraudulent at worst. The resulting mash of overlapping and competing ideas provides, not clarity, but massive amounts of confusion in the pursuit of validating (or invalidating) project management science ideas, hypotheses and theories.

This chapter examines how commonly-held precepts in the body of management science are advanced, and offers a basis for evaluating their validity. The result, I hope, will be a Kuhnian paradigm shift in the way project management is perceived as fulfilling a specific role within the macroeconomic environment.

The Uneven Advancement of Project Management Theory

In the nano sciences, the ability to characterise the shape of a given material at the molecular level is extremely important. Unfortunately, the technology that would allow a direct observation of materials' molecular shape has yet to be discovered. However, neutron science does have a way of allowing *indirect* observations to be made. It works like this: while a given molecule's shape can't be observed, special equipment does allow the behaviour of interacting neutrons to be directly observed. By bombarding a target material with a neutron stream, and observing the behaviour of those neutrons, it is possible to characterise the target material. A rough analogy would be that it's possible to get an idea of what the invisible man looks like without touching him by bouncing ping pong balls off his face and noting the exact points where the balls change direction.

In the management sciences it's often difficult or impossible to quantify, or even observe, the impact of a given business tactic or stratagem, due to the vast numbers of influencing factors involved in the economic environment. For example, when the Project Management Institute (PMI) was founded in 1969, its ideas represented a profound challenge to much of the conventional wisdom then-prevalent in management science circles, whether its founders realised it or not. Many of their theoretical insights had been already borne out in thousands of real-world 'experiments' which, while not being able to isolate the specific impacts of a rather broad set of technical approaches, nevertheless showed the macro set of project management ideas to be sufficiently valid to justify widespread adoption by those organisations that both performed project work and wanted (or needed) to perform better than their competitors.

These ideas represented a challenge to the widely-held notion that the ultimate goal of all management is to 'maximise shareholder wealth'. With their focus on scope, cost and schedule – parameters that, if not pointedly set by the customer, are at least directly relevant to achieving organisational goals – PMI® had posited an entirely different technical approach to management success. However, when a certain set of theories of how management ought to work cannot be evaluated empirically, they are typically furthered or embraced through one of two routes:

- the theory set has a direct (positive) causal effect on the organisation's goals (typically maximising profit is predominant); or else

- the government mandates its use.

Generally Accepted Accounting Principles (GAAP) are universally employed because they enjoy major pushes from both of these drivers. They represent the main information stream for guiding business decisions, while also providing the basis for governments to assess and collect taxes. The body of knowledge associated with project management has enjoyed a lesser level of implementation push. The earliest versions of codified project management, the Cost/Schedule Control System Criterion (C/SCSC), were required of all contractors working on major projects for the United States Department of Defense. But as far as having a direct impact on a given organisation's profitability, the results were mixed. Some industries, like construction, already relied heavily on the Critical Path Method (CPM) of scheduling, but usually had little need for the risk management techniques advanced by PMI®. The pharmaceutical industry based many of their business decisions on the information stream emanating from their risk management systems (though those systems little resemble the ones recommended in the *PMBOK® Guide*), but had little need for Earned Value Management Systems (EVMs). Earned Value Systems are rather common in the manufacturing industry where advanced scope management systems are often superfluous. So, whereas virtually all components of GAAP are universally incorporated (it simply wouldn't do to have, say, accounts receivable be GAAP compliant, while payroll is not), the various elements that make up the complete body of project management theory are far more compartmentalised, depending on the organisations' specific circumstances. This compartmentalisation, while rendering direct observations of project management's effectiveness impossible, does allow indirect observations.

The uneven advancement of project management theory as a whole tends to highlight project management's overall weakness. Organisations embracing the whole of the project management body of knowledge, as documented by the PMI, could not demonstrate a consistent competitive advantage over those organisations that chose to only implement certain aspects of project management, or even none at all. Not to state the obvious, but if there were a direct cause and effect relationship between an organisation embracing the totality of project management theory and a verifiable jump in profitability, there would be no need for all of those articles, papers and webinars, touting the advantages of embracing project management techniques. There simply aren't any articles in, say, the chemists' trade journals, touting the advantages of using Bunsen burners – their utility is obvious. The very existence of such articles, papers and webinars (many of which take on an insufferable eat-your-peas style of hectoring tone) points out the fact that project management theory, taken as a whole, has failed to conclusively demonstrate its ability to impart in its practitioners a consistent competitive advantage in any given industry.

Now, is this to say that project management techniques, taken as a whole, are invalid? No, not at all – but I am saying that the current state of project management theory, as described in the PMI®'s *PMBOK® Guide*, is not articulated in a cohesive, consistent structure. As I describe in my recently-released book *Game Theory in Management* (2012) the various chapters of the *PMBOK® Guide* are written as if the authors were unable or unwilling to define the limits of the specific techniques and approaches they were describing. If the *PMBOK® Guide* was a colouring book, with nine areas intended to be filled in with nine different colours, then the result looks as if none of the lines were respected, and all of the crayon-wielders attempted to claim much more of the theoretical whole than they should have. Given this mismash of overly extended, overlapping management theories, is it any wonder that project management, taken as a whole, still requires massive marketing efforts to gain universal acceptance?

The Coming Sea-Change

While pretending to be able to quantify how the future will unfold is the risk analysts' folly, I would like to offer speculation on how project management theory, as an encapsulated whole, will fare in the years to come. As theory advocates and *PMBOK® Guide* chapter writing and review committees churn out ideas on how they *think* management ought to operate, the free marketplace will continue to put into place those ideas that work (or those that organisations think will work), and eschew those that do not have a positive impact on the profit-and-loss statement. (I fully anticipate that one of the earliest casualties of this process will be much of what passes for modern risk management theory, being the waste of time that it is.) These two bodies of knowledge are destined to become casual adversaries, identifiable by how they are embraced by managers: the one set will be readily adopted and employed, the other implemented only by the intellectual equivalent of academic nagging, with its data needed for no other purpose than the attainment of a professional certification or for compliance issues. And therein lies an irony: as the gulf between the two bodies of management science – real world and theoretical – grow apart, the value of those certifications to their recipients will erode, and rapidly. Organisations intent on maximising profit (virtually all of them) will begin to recognise applicants with project management certifications as potentially knowing a bunch of stuff that just isn't so, or has minimal application(s) in their specific industry, diminishing any advantage that the applicants perceive they gain by spending the time and energy in attaining the certification.

Oh, the mainstream professional organisations advocating traditional project management or cost engineering will muddle along for a while, propped up by the occasional government head-fake towards endorsing them, their standards or their certifications, but the free marketplace will remain unfooled. The sea-change will come when a professional organisation, with a clear vision of the valid capabilities of the business tactics and techniques of project management – as well as their limitations – gains prominence, and can not only articulate their value, but can demonstrate it in the marketplace. This vision requires the identification of the lines of demarcation separating the realms of asset, project and strategic management, and where the techniques and approaches germane to each of these arenas have efficacy, and, more importantly, where they do not. The natural enemies of such a professional organisation are advocates for specific business theoretical approaches, who have advanced their pet management theories and techniques by encoding them as 'best business practices' in documents that make up industry standards, such as the *PMBOK® Guide*, or ISO 9000 (Quality). Whether or not one of the existing, prominent project management organisations changes course and achieves this or a new upstart fills that role is anyone's guess, though I wouldn't bet on any of the existing bodies. Their committees' needs for diversity and consensus, added to their inability to recognise the inherent intellectual inconsistency inherent in fulfilling both those needs simultaneously, essentially guarantee that sharp course corrections never occur, no matter how obviously appropriate.

What will precipitate this coming sea-change? Managers continuing to do what they do, regardless of what the professional institutes and standards-writers say they ought to do. As the rest of us watch this epistemological gulf grow, I believe it likely that those who advocate for certain out-of-favour technical approaches will become more shrill in their papers and presentations, as well as their efforts to have governments require their list of project management recommendations be implemented. Conversely, those managers who consistently meet or exceed their portfolio managers' and organisations' goals, while maintaining the latitude to pick and choose which aspects of the whole of project management theory they employ, will point the way to which parts of the project management body of knowledge ought to be imitated, and which should be discarded. It's my belief that the soon-to-be discarded set is much larger than anyone currently suspects.

And that's why there's a sea-change coming in project management.

References

Hatfield, Michael (2012). *Game theory in Management*, Farnham: Gower Publishing.

Kuhn, Thomas (1962). *The Structure of Scientific Revolutions*, Chicago: University of Chicago Press.

21

Senior Management
From Projects to Strategy, and Back Again

Darren Dalcher

One of the key success factors for project management revolves around the availability of support and buy-in from senior management. Reports on project success and failure typically emphasise executive support as a distinguishing and necessary ingredient. Embedding major improvement initiatives, such as maturity models and process improvement schemes, into an organisation also depends on harnessing support at a strategic level which is often identified as a critical pre-requisite to the success of such initiatives. Indeed, most attempts to introduce and embed change at an organisational level would depend on the availability of leaders willing to engage, defend, support and champion the initiatives to ensure they survive and thrive.

The discipline is increasingly aware of the need to 'sell' project management to corporate executives. In a landmark study published in 2002, Professor Janice Thomas and her colleagues asked why it was so difficult to convince senior executives of the importance of project management. Their Project Management Institute (PMI) study confirms that many project managers pitch the profession too low by focusing on the tactical importance of projects. Senior executives, however, are looking for a more strategic focus, concerned with the long-term delivery of value. The study notes that successful sellers emphasise the alignment of project management with corporate strategy and goals and distinct value statements. Ultimately senior executives want to understand the benefits that project management can offer in their particular context.

A number of chapters, including the last one, hinted that the theory of project management might be flawed, suggesting alternative ways of looking at how to deliver projects. It might be that the discipline is partly at fault for failing to transmit the correct message. Describing a project as a temporary endeavour with start and end points, might well be doing the discipline a disservice, by ignoring the need to focus on benefits, the alignment with corporate objectives, the focus on sustainability and the strategic and organisational context. Presenting projects as a temporary group activity or as the allocation of resources also misses the wider purpose and goal, and more crucially ignores the link to upper-level values, priorities and concerns that are likely to be of interest to senior executives.

The depiction of project management as a simplistic approach that can be executed in six quick steps available in a DIY self-help style book, or the random allocation of the title of project manager in shows such as *The Apprentice* may also be underselling the promise of project management. Recent conversations with senior executives have suggested that the impression of an execution-focused tactical undertaking seems to resonate with their experiences of the discipline and what it can offer. In order to sell project management to senior executives, professionals would need to use the right language, set the right expectations and have the right level of conversation.

Within the discipline of project management one increasingly hears about the new world and the new challenges that are encountered. One of the key challenges is to embed project management successfully in organisations. The chapter by Antonio Nieto-Rodriguez gives an encouragement for rethinking the role and value of project management. His chapter attempts to make sense of the way project management is perceived by looking at the views of some of the most recognised management gurus, the leading MBA programmes and the leading management publications. His conclusion is that project management needs to become more relevant to the concerns of senior leaders in order to justify its inclusion and reverse its apparent invisibility and absence.

The contribution is extracted from Antonio's book *The Focused Organization: How Concentrating on a Few Key Initiatives Can Dramatically Improve Strategy Execution* published by Gower. The book makes a persuasive case for fewer and more effectively selected and managed projects that will form the key to strategic and long-term success in organisations. By focusing on a number of key initiatives, organisations can perform significantly better than unfocused organisations, delivering improved performance that translates into the delivery of strategic objectives, motivated staff and financial benefits. The book will challenge project managers to look at organisations through two very different dimensions, which need to be balanced to deliver successful strategy execution.

Perhaps the two key contributions of the work are in posing the searching questions (and providing a set of potential answers) and in offering a new vocabulary that can underpin a new culture and support the conversation with senior executives to ensure that project management can be rightly viewed as an essential and effective strategic discipline.

The Chinese military strategist and philosopher Sun Tzu noted that, 'All men can see these tactics whereby I conquer, but what none can see is the strategy out of which victory is evolved.' The conversation required to successfully embed project management within organisations needs to be informed by a recognition of the strategic objectives, values and preferences of organisations so that outcomes can better reflect strategic objectives. By joining the conversation, project management can become a meaningful partner in strategic execution and corporate value delivery, and in the process obtain senior strategic support and perhaps begin to improve its track record of delivery, the underlying expectations in senior circles, and the perception and visibility of the discipline. Indeed, as the discipline seeks to move from doing to shaping, it must embrace a greater focus on objectives, intentions and purpose, and begin to enact a perspective of active, responsible and effective project leadership, rather than mere and efficient project execution or passive management.

References

Thomas, Janice, Delise, Connie L. and Jugdev, Kam (2002). *Selling Project Management to Senior Executives: Framing the Moves that Matter*. Newtown Square, PA: PMI.

Evidence of the Neglect of Project Management by Senior Executives

Antonio Nieto-Rodriguez

The Origins of Current Views of Project Management

I have spent the last ten years trying to understand why senior executives seem to neither understand project management nor regard it as an important means of strategy execution. While conducting my research, I discovered that most heads of organisations view project management as a highly technical discipline – an area for engineers and IT professionals. Consequently, they:

- lack a basic understanding of how to link each of their strategic projects with the company's overall strategy;

- do not devote much time to developing project management competencies in-house;

- fail to implement a formal project selection process and investment committee, which discusses, prioritises and decides on all the new project proposals;

- lack the means to monitor the success or failure of their strategic projects.

But why do so many senior executives feel this way? In an attempt to get to the deeper reasons for their views, I sought answers to the following questions:

1. Do the theories of the most highly regarded business management gurus, those that influence the way businesses are managed (for example, Taylor, Drucker and Porter), mention project management and/or the importance of its link with strategy execution?

2. Have the top business schools, those that train most senior executives and future leaders, been teaching the value of project management and its link with strategy execution?

3. Is project management regularly discussed in the finest business publications?

Disregarded by Business Management Gurus

My rationale for scrutinising the work of the so-called business management gurus is that they have shaped the way companies do business today. Their theories have promoted big waves of change and improvement for many decades and have become obligatory reading for most business school students.

I looked at business management experts of the twentieth and early twenty-first centuries whom I considered to be the most influential. My aim was to first understand the impact of their theories on business and then to determine whether they discussed project management as a discipline and/or its link to strategy execution.

I describe below three out of the 11 management gurus and its theories that I researched.

Frederick Winslow Taylor (20 March 1856–21 March 1915)

SUMMARY OF KEY PREMISES

Considered the father of scientific management, Frederick Winslow Taylor sought to improve industrial efficiency by systematically breaking tasks down into their component elements in an effort to find the one best way to complete them. He is well-known for his time-and-motion studies, which involved using a stopwatch to time a worker's sequence of motions, eliminating unnecessary motions, and then determining how the task could be performed more efficiently.

During the industrial age, scientific management changed the way companies looked at production. Industrial plants and factories, in particular, launched initiatives to improve production efficiencies. These initiatives can be viewed as projects, since they were time limited and independent of daily operations. In fact, each of the four points in Taylor's principles of scientific management was a project by itself: the scientific study/analysis, the training, the implementation of detailed instructions and the equal allocation of work between workers and managers.

Thus, Taylor's theories, without mentioning it, led to a significant increase in an organisation's project activity. But this increase was just temporary; once the improvements in the production processes were made, the companies returned to their operations to run the businesses activities.

MENTION OF PROJECT MANAGEMENT AND ITS LINK WITH STRATEGY EXECUTION

Although applying Taylor's theories increased the number of projects in organisations, these theories neither talked about project management or its value nor linked it with strategy execution.

Igor Ansoff (12 December 1918–14 July 2002)

As the pioneer of strategic management, Igor Ansoff developed a unique set of theories based on analyses of his predecessors' work combined with his own insights into the variables that contribute to successful strategies.

Prior to the publication in 1965 of Ansoff's landmark book *Corporate Strategy*, companies lacked guidance on how to plan for the future. Traditionally, they developed a budget and projected it several years into the future but paid little attention to strategic and execution issues. Ansoff stressed in his book that in a business environment characterised by growing competition – an increase in mergers, acquisitions, and diversification – and mounting turbulence, it was essential to anticipate future challenges and to draw up appropriate strategies to respond to these challenges.

Ansoff's strategic management theories had a twofold impact on the number of projects at most companies. At first, companies formed strategy departments and began to implement Ansoff's teachings through new projects.

During this first wave, the primary entities that benefited were consulting companies, which used Ansoff's concepts to advise businesses in developing their strategies.

In the 1970s and 1980s, when the establishment of strategic planning departments was very popular, companies significantly increased their projects. One reason for this upsurge was that strategic planning created greater transparency, allowing companies to have a better view of the different initiatives and translating into more projects.

However, companies quickly encountered trouble because the strategic planning process did not cover how to execute multiple projects. At this point, the gap between strategy planning and strategy execution widened and became bigger and bigger every year.

MENTION OF PROJECT MANAGEMENT AND ITS LINK WITH STRATEGY EXECUTION

As mentioned above, at first Ansoff's theories increased organisations' projects only slightly. Once the new strategic development offices were created, however, the number of projects exploded. Ansoff does mention the concept of programmes, but he neither expands on it nor explains the link between project management and strategy execution.

Michael Eugene Porter (23 May 1947–)

Michael Porter has been identified by many surveys as the world's most influential thinker on management and competitiveness. He is the founder of the modern strategy field, and his work has redefined theories about competitiveness, economic development, economically distressed urban communities, environmental policy and the role of corporations in society.

Porter changed the way companies look at their businesses and analyse their strategies. However, his theories did not significantly increase the number of projects. Through his value-chain concept, he enforced the functional structure of companies, which has become a key challenge for organisations if they want to be able to execute their strategic projects.

MENTION OF PROJECT MANAGEMENT AND ITS LINK WITH STRATEGY EXECUTION

Porter does not mention either the importance of project management or the link with strategy execution. Despite the fact that he revolutionised the way companies look at strategy, he surprisingly fails to cover how strategy is executed.

Summary

None of the most influential business management gurus referred to project management as an important business methodology or as a critical component of strategy execution. This neglect is one of the main reasons why most of today's business leaders continue to ignore the value of project management.

Ignored by Most Top MBA Programmes

After determining that most business management gurus disregard project management and its link with strategy execution, I wanted to find out whether the same was true at the top business schools. Specifically, I wanted know whether the MBA programmes at such world-renowned institutions as Harvard and INSEAD, which teach the world's future CEOs and senior executives, actually include project management as part of their core business curriculum.

Masters in Business Administration (MBA) programmes have an extraordinary reputation and openly claim that they 'help you to develop a leadership mindset and strong foundation of management skills to succeed in your first job and throughout your career. We prepare you for the future. We empower you to make the difference'.[1]

Over the past 40 years, the MBA has become one of the most sought-after degrees in the world. Many of the current top managers have gone through this business programme, and most future leaders will do so. The traditional MBA programme has a duration of between 12 and 24 months, and it is divided into two blocks. The first block is composed of core courses, which are mandatory for every student. The second block comprises an extensive list of elective courses, from which students select a certain number that relate to their specialisation.

---

1   http://www.gsb.stanford.edu/mba/.

Research into the Inclusion of Project Management Courses

Using the *Financial Times* 2010 ranking of the world's top business schools,[2] I researched whether any of them taught project management as either a core course or an elective. Table 21.1 shows the results of my research.

Table 21.1   Project management as a discipline in top business schools

SL. No	School Name	Country	Core Project or Programme Management	Electives Project or Programme
1	London Business School	UK	No	Yes
2	University of Pennsylvania: Wharton	USA	No	No
3	Harvard Business School	USA	No	No
4	Stanford University GSB	USA	No	No
5	INSEAD	France/Singapore	No	No
6	Columbia Business School	USA	No	No
7	IE Business School	Spain	No	No
8	MIT Sloan School of Management	USA	No	No
9	University of Chicago: Booth	USA	No	No
10	Hong Kong UST Business School	China	No	No
11	Iese Business School	Spain	No	No
12	Indian School of Business	India	No	No
13	New York University: Stern	USA	No	No
14	Dartmouth College: Tuck	USA	No	No
15	IMD	Switzerland	No	No
16	Yale School of Management	USA	No	No
17	University of Oxford: Said	UK	No	No
18	HEC Paris	France	No	No
19	Esade Business School	Spain	No	No
20	Duke University: Fuqua	USA	No	No
21	University of Cambridge: Judge	UK	No	No
22	Ceibs	China	No	Yes
23	Northwestern University: Kellogg	USA	No	No
24	Lancaster University Management School	UK	No	No
25	Rotterdam School of Management, Erasmus University	Netherlands	No	No

---

2   I performed my research during the autumn of 2010.

The results are astonishing: only two of the top 100 MBA programmes in the world teach project management as a core course. The first business school that required its students to take a course in project management is the UK's Cranfield School of Management,[3] which is ranked 26th in the world. The second and last business school that teaches project management as a mandatory course is the University of Iowa's Tippie[4] College of Business, ranked 64th in the world.

I strongly believe that by 2020, most of the MBA programmes in the world will offer project management as an elective class. A bit more time will be required for project management to become a mandatory course, primarily because it will need to be adapted to the MBA programme and its unique way of being taught.

Discounted as a Key Topic by the Finest Business Publications

Despite all of my findings indicating that project management has been ignored, I decided to complete one last piece of research before drawing conclusions. This involved reviewing *McKinsey Quarterly* and *Harvard Business Review* to see how these top business publications cover the topic of project management and its link with strategy execution.

First I looked at *McKinsey Quarterly*, which was founded in 1964 by McKinsey and Company and is targeted to chief executives, top managers and selected academics. Its articles are written by McKinsey consultants to offer practical suggestions culled from their experience with the world's largest companies. Initially, the *Quarterly* was distributed by the McKinsey partners but is now distributed electronically.

Reviewing the list of functions on the electronic version of the *McKinsey Quarterly*, I noticed many familiar ones but none related to project management or strategy execution. Does this mean that these two topics are not sufficiently relevant?

---

3   http://www.som.cranfield.ac.uk/som/p786/Programmes-and-Executive-Development/MBA/
     your-mba-programme/The-Cranfield-MBA-Programme-structure.
4   http://tippie.uiowa.edu/fulltimemba/academics/corecourses.cfm.

Second, I looked at the *Harvard Business Review*,[5] the bible in terms of business management thinking and new trends. First published in 1992 by Harvard University, its mission is to improve the practice of project management and its impact on changing the world. In 2010, the *Review* had a circulation of 236,000.

Reviewing the publication's website to determine the topics mentioned and the number of references to each topic, this is what I found (Table 21.2):

Table 21.2   Number of references/articles per topic, *Harvard Business Review* (3 July 2011)

	Business Theories		
	Author	**Refer to Project Management**	**Link Strategy and Execution**
1	Henry Ford	No	No
2	Frederick Winslow Taylor	No	No
3	Peter Drucker	No	No
4	Michael Eugene Porter	No	No
5	Deming	No	No
6	Mintzberg	No	No
7	Prahalad and Hamel	No	No
8	Hammer and Champy	No	No
9	Kotter and Schlesigner	Yes	No
10	Kaplan and Norton	No	No
11	Kruger	No	No

Clearly, the key topics written about in the *Harvard Business Review* are the ones most addressed by business gurus, which in turn are the subjects taught most frequently at the top business schools and discussed most often by leading consultants. Only 432 *Harvard Business Review* articles have been written about project management, which represent less than 0.50% of the total number of articles published. Strategy execution – or implementation, as the publication calls it – is the subject of a somewhat greater number of articles (1,203); but both topics are far from the top of the list.

---

5   http://www.hbr.com.

Conclusions

My research shows very clearly why project management has not been relevant and explains the consequent disregard of this discipline by senior leaders. For most of the project management community this is a very painful discovery; but it helps to understand the reasons for this indifference. For many strategists, this lack of awareness of the importance of project management explains the problems with strategy execution. Only when project management is recognised as being vital to strategy execution will companies begin to more effectively achieve their goals.

References

Ansoff, Igor (1965). *Corporate Strategy: Business Policy for Growth and Expansion,* New York: McGraw-Hill.

Summary
Project Management Research: The Long Journey

Darren Dalcher

The book has covered an enormous array of topics and areas, highlighting the diversity and vitality of project management research and practice, and the need to widen the perspective of what may be encompassed by the management and leadership of projects.

Project management is a core competence required to deliver change measured in terms of achieving desired outcomes with associated benefits. With projects increasingly viewed as managing the change efforts of society, project management is called upon to cross functional, organisational and societal boundaries and handle the inherent complexity and uncertainty required to bring about a new reality. Indeed, one of the key themes that emerge from many of the discussions in the individual chapters is the need to engage with uncertainty, complexity and ambiguity.

Project managers often act as agents of change translating wish, fantasy and fancy into a delivered reality. In a world characterised by demanding constraints, growing expectations and conflicting tradeoffs, managers balance priorities, needs and potential. Their continuing ability to deliver, transform and innovate make their achievements a triumph, proving that project management can become the art of the possible.

Yet, project managers are continuously challenged to deliver more with less whilst improving the track record of project delivery. Fresh insights into how people and teams work, how to lead in complex and dynamic environments and how to improve delivery capability continue to emerge in different areas and domains. They demonstrate the potential for deriving new ways of working and making sense of project contexts and environments.

The project context is increasingly becoming more encompassing and more intensive. New technologies open up new possibilities, requiring new ways of working. The challenges seem more demanding and the impacts of our decisions appear more critical to our ultimate survival. These challenges require fundamentally new ways of making sense and shaping a world we can neither fully control, nor fully understand.

Is project management ready for this new world? The scale and complexity of issues we are facing is on the rise. Indeed it would appear that the new project management would need to address the wider concerns of a more engaged, more global and better-informed society. Yet, we are also faced with a period of greater austerity and an increased focus on accountability.

Another theme that emerges from the different discussions is the need to move from managing to leading. Managing is the hallmark of a more certain and more control-oriented strategy, while leadership points to a different and more varied skillset. Lack of control and a greater reliance on a network of participants requires a more organic approach that emphasises influence, participation and collaboration. Gradual exploration can therefore be guided by vision and purpose that can help in forming and confirming the direction of travel.

Success in the future would require better understanding of the context and deeper engagement with the business. It will also imply an acute understanding of the values and preferences of different, yet much wider circles of stakeholders communities, possibly arranged in complex and interconnected ecologies. The set of concerns is likely to encompass sustainability and survivability issues, extended time horizons and considerations of wider communities of interest. The old tools and approaches that characterise the pioneering mindsets that shaped project management will require adjusting to encompass new ways of balancing ethical, economic and environmental considerations, and reflect a changing understanding of the economic mechanisms that underpin engineering and development activities from a humanistic perspective.

This book offers the collated and narrated beginnings of a discussion on how to achieve more with less. As we dare to become more ambitious, we will need to leverage our insights and understanding and develop new ways of addressing the emerging challenges. In doing so we may discover that sharing across boundaries and silos will enrich and refresh our metaphors, tools, perspectives and values – so that they can support and underpin our continuing journeys in both chartered and unchartered territory, as we endeavour to learn to deal with change over time.

> *We shall never cease from exploration*
> *And the end of all our exploring*
> *Will be to arrive where we started*
> *And know it for the first time.*
>
> T.S. Elliot, Little Gidding

Index

Accountability 137, 139, 140, 161, 222
Active ownership 188, 191
Agents of change 221
Ambiguity 3, 4, 31, 39, 40, 42, 128, 221
Ansoff, Igor 213–4
Association for Project Management
    51, 64, 107, 179

Behavioural competences 111
Benefit shortfall 159–160
Benefits 2, 3, 4, 11, 20, 24, 27, 34, 39–46,
    113, 116, 155–62, 187, 208, 221
Benefits forecasting 158, 160–2
Benefits management 43, 44, 156, 160
Benefits realisation 45, 46, 155–6,
    157–62
Bernstein, Peter 131, 133
Black swans 195
Body of knowledge 21, 64, 107, 125,
    145–7, 179, 197, 198, 203, 204,
    206
Bohm 103, 104
Bohmian dialogue 102–3
Budget 29, 56, 64, 67–95, 110, 111, 115,
    117, 129, 130, 132, 136, 137, 140,
    157, 161, 185, 213
Business case 15, 20, 35, 45, 131, 141,
    142, 155, 157–161
Business development 17–19
Business strategy 47

Change 39–40, 41, 43, 46, 56, 115, 117,
    118, 136, 138, 140, 143, 146, 149,
    150, 155, 156, 157, 161, 180, 188,
    189, 193, 195, 197, 207, 221, 223
Change initiatives 39, 156, 157, 161
Change leaders 45
Change management 126, 146, 147,
    149, 153, 157
Chaos 54–5, 56
Client 17, 18, 19, 42, 94, 107, 110–111,
    124, 129, 145
Cognitive biases 156, 157–9, 160, 162
Cognitive mapping 18
Collaboration 188, 191, 192, 194, 222
Communication 20, 21, 60, 61, 99,
    102–3, 104, 109, 111, 145, 146,
    147, 149, 153, 173, 174, 175,
    179–181, 183–186, 197
Compliance 17, 34, 35, 38, 205
Competent project manager 110–112
Complexity 3, 4, 19, 40, 50, 53, 54, 55,
    56, 60, 120, 127–8, 129, 130, 131,
    133, 136, 140, 143, 180, 221, 222
Conflict 33, 50, 108, 111, 146, 158, 179,
    197
Conflict management 151
Context 4, 6, 11, 16, 18, 28, 30, 108,
    116, 127, 128, 135, 136, 141, 147,
    166, 179, 184, 185, 187, 188, 192,
    207, 208, 222

Contextual competences 111

Contract 19, 21, 60, 117, 123, 124, 128, 130, 133

Contractor 94, 110, 121, 124, 203

Cooperation 172–3

Core competence 2, 221

Cost 4, 28, 34, 56, 64, 67, 68, 69, 71, 72, 73, 95, 96, 102, 109, 111, 113, 133, 155, 156, 158, 159, 160, 162, 179, 185, 186, 202, 203, 205

Cost engineering 205

Creativity 98, 99, 103–4, 129, 130

Critical Success Factors (CSFs) 30, 61, 142

Decision making 1, 12, 15, 23, 31, 33, 39, 43, 54, 65, 107, 116, 127, 136, 146, 152, 155, 165, 166, 167, 169, 171, 172, 174, 176, 192

Decisions 6, 7, 12, 15, 16, 17, 23, 31, 35, 40, 52, 59, 63, 64, 99, 102, 108, 110, 122, 131, 136, 140, 156, 162, 165–7, 169, 171, 172, 173, 174, 176, 181, 188, 198, 203, 222

Deliverables 34, 102, 115, 122, 124, 169, 189

Delphi technique 162

Early finish problem 77–9

Earned schedule 64, 67, 79–84

Earned value 63–96

Enterprise risk management 24, 28

EQ 59–60, 97

ERP 123

Esprit de corps 101–2

Ethical dilemmas 108

Ethics 1, 98, 107–8, 109–112, 140, 143

EVM 63–96

Expectations 19, 24, 34, 56, 102, 107, 108, 113, 114, 122, 145, 152, 155, 156, 157, 179, 180, 181, 185, 186, 197, 208, 209, 221

Feedback 54, 186, 192, 193

Forecasts 68, 157, 158, 159, 160, 161, 162

Gateway review 125

Global orientation 3, 4, 139, 141, 159, 193, 222

Governance 1, 31–32, 33–38, 43, 44, 131, 143,

Governance paradigms 35
    Agile pragmatist 34–5
    Conformist 34–5
    Flexible economist 34–5
    Versatile artist 34–5

Greenleaf, Robert 100–101

Harvard Business Review 218

Hero project managers 130

High performance teams 102, 151, 172, 173–4

Hypothesis 188, 201

Ill-structured problems 49

Illusion of project stability, the 10

Innovation 98, 191, 192, 195

Inspiration 57, 97–8, 103, 116, 131

Intuition 51, 53, 56, 98, 131, 175

IPMA Competence Baseline (ICB) 108

IQ 59–60, 97

ISO 26000 139

Iterative planning 11

Judgement 29, 30, 49, 60, 61, 93, 102, 103, 106, 169, 171

Judgement under stress 172

Known unknowns 7

Kuhn, Thomas 201

Late finish problem 73–6

Leader 5, 20, 21, 45, 57–8, 100, 101, 103, 130, 132, 166, 175, 181, 193, 207, 208, 212

Leadership 1, 20, 49, 55, 56, 57–61, 98, 99, 100, 109, 111, 129, 132, 133, 145, 146, 150, 161, 169–176, 180, 215, 222

Leadership competence 59–61

Lean 132

Learning 43, 45, 46, 55, 56, 61, 101, 128, 129, 131, 133, 142, 188, 191–195

Limits to growth 138

Linear 13, 45, 49, 53, 54, 56, 103, 121, 127, 195

Liquidated damages 132

Long-term 39, 45, 59, 95, 131, 135, 139, 140 141, 146, 188, 189, 191, 192, 193, 194, 207, 208

Materials 121, 122, 123, 124, 126, 142

MBA 215–7

McKinsey Quarterly 217

Meaning 100, 170, 183, 184, 185, 198

Measures 36, 63, 67, 72, 133

Messy problems 1, 50, 53–4

Methodology 10, 34, 36, 38, 43, 215

Milestone 63, 93, 125, 169

Miscommunication 185

Modified schedule performance index 85–95

More with less 4, 221, 222

Motivation 60, 131, 147, 151

MQ 59–60

New world 3, 4, 5, 208, 222

Obeng, Eddie 3

OECD, see Organisation for Economic Co-operation and Development

Office of Government Commerce 157

OODA (Observe, Orient, Decide, Act) loop 11

Opportunity 13, 17, 28, 29, 30, 44, 56, 57, 143, 195

Organisation for Economic Co-operation and Development 32

Organisational change 43, 60, 61, 149, 153

Organisational learning 22, 142

Outcome 2, 13, 24, 34, 35, 39, 40, 41, 46, 56, 64, 101, 124, 130, 132, 136, 158, 185, 187, 191, 209, 221

Outcome management 128

Outsourcing 124

Outsourcing risk 130

Paradigm shift 201

Performance management 122, 126

Performance measurement 1, 64, 67

Plan 10, 11, 12, 13, 19, 20, 27, 29, 41, 56, 59, 64, 111, 115, 120, 121–4, 125, 126, 132, 153, 158, 159, 161, 162, 175, 179, 184, 192, 195,

Planning steered evaluation 191–2

PMI 51, 59, 111, 125, 202, 203, 204, 207

PMO 35, 37

Politics 56, 97, 145, 197

Porter, Michael Eugene 214–5

Positive stress 170–171

Post project review 29

Practice 120, 128, 146, 193, 198, 221

Preference engineering 131

Problem solving 1, 49–50, 103, 127

Procurement 111, 122, 123, 124, 126, 142

Professional associations 6, 107, 202, 204, 205

Professional virtues 112

Professionalism 36, 107–8, 110, 130,
    136, 143
Programme 1, 7, 15, 24, 28, 32, 35,
    36, 56, 111, 128, 156, 159, 188,
    191–195, 214
    Emergent 42
    Vision-led 42
Programme governance 44
Programme management 1, 35, 36,
    37, 39–47, 53
Programme management life cycle
    45–6
Progress 63, 64, 68, 70, 71, 84, 125,
    142, 145
Project context 141, 222
Project delivery chain 122, 124
Project failure 32, 145, 179, 187, 197, 211
Project governance 31–38
Project initiation 192
Project integration 122, 124–6
Project leadership, see leadership
Project management governance 37
Project Management Office, see PMO
Project organisation 126, 142, 188,
    191, 194, 195
Project planning chain 121–2, 122–4
Project portfolio management 35, 36,
    155–6
Project psychology 145–153
Project reporting 142
Project reviews 22
Project risk attributes 18, 19
Project risk map 18, 19
Project stakeholder, see Stakeholder
Project start 15, 93
Project success 60, 61, 122, 141, 150,
    185, 207
Project team, see Team
Punitive contractual sanctions 130
Purpose 45, 99, 100, 129, 208, 209

Quality 56, 109, 111, 121, 122, 124,
    125, 126, 179, 193, 205

Reference class forecasting 162
Relationships 32, 35, 44, 97, 111, 114,
    115, 116, 119, 120, 133, 136, 149,
    151, 194
Repertory Grid Technique 18
Resource consumption 70, 71
Resources 9, 17, 19, 20, 30, 33, 35, 41,
    44, 56, 60, 70, 71, 72, 92, 93, 94,
    111, 120, 121, 122, 124, 126, 132,
    133, 136, 138, 139, 142, 171, 179,
    187, 208
Responsibility 45, 101, 110, 135–6,
    137–143, 146, 173, 189, 192,
    193
Return on Investment 33, 131, 157
Reviews 17, 22, 29, 36, 122, 125, 126,
    161–2
Risk 1, 4, 7, 9, 17, 18, 23–30, 49, 52,
    103, 111, 119, 130, 152, 159, 173,
    180, 181, 185, 204
    Qualitative 52–3
    Quantitative 52–3
Risk energetics 30
Risk leadership 55–6
Risk management 7, 9, 17–22, 23–24,
    26–30, 42, 51–56, 68, 93–4, 96,
    142, 152, 180, 203
    People 29–30
    Persistence 30
    Principles 28
    Process 28–9

Satisficing 54
Scenarios 13, 52, 56, 77, 84
Schedule 28, 210, 123, 133, 137, 169,
    179, 185, 202
Schedule performance index 67, 73–9

Scope 56, 64, 68, 69, 70, 71, 77, 78, 93, 94, 111, 137, 140, 142, 143, 179, 185, 202, 203

Scope shift 143

Selection 124, 142, 150, 194, 211

Selling project management 207

Servant leader 100–101

Shareholder 33, 34, 137, 160,202

Short-term 95, 125, 127, 131, 135, 139, 140, 141, 188

Situational competencies 60–61

Spirit 101–2

Spirituality 99–105

Sponsor 5, 18, 19, 34, 41, 45, 46, 47, 61, 115, 116, 122, 137, 140, 143, 160, 181

Sponsorship 111

SQ 98

Stakeholder 3, 4, 19, 20, 33–34, 43, 44, 45, 46, 50, 52, 54, 56, 59, 84, 97, 99, 100, 102, 113–118, 120, 121, 122, 125, 126, 130, 135, 136, 137, 139, 140, 141, 145, 151, 152, 153, 155, 169, 173, 175, 179, 180, 181, 183, 185, 186, 188, 222

Stakeholder analysis 20

Stakeholder engagement 139, 152

Stakeholder management 21, 43, 44, 115, 116, 118, 181

Stakeholder's stakeholders 116–7

Strategic decisions 15, 17, 39, 43

Strategic misrepresentation 160

Strategy 3, 16, 19, 33, 41, 44, 45, 46, 47, 137, 138, 165, 175, 193, 195, 207, 209, 211–19

Strategy execution 211–219

Strategy implementation 22

Stress 2, 166, 169–76

Subcontractors 4

Success 4, 5, 8, 13, 15, 28, 39, 45, 59, 60, 61, 113, 114, 121, 122, 123, 124, 127, 130, 131, 141, 145, 149, 155, 158, 162, 185, 187–9, 207, 211, 222

Sunk costs 131

Supply Chain Council 119

Supply chains 119–126

Supporting competencies 60–61

Supportive evaluation model 192

Sustainability 1, 4, 124, 126, 135–143, 146, 187–9

Sustainable change 146, 191–195

Sustainable development 140

Tame problems 49, 50, 53, 54, 55

Taylor, Frederick Winslow 212–3

Team 20, 21, 30, 42, 56, 59, 61, 97–8, 99–104, 116, 142, 145, 149–150, 173–176

Team building 151

Team development 99

Team dynamics 151

Team meeting 125

Team selection 149–50

Technical competences 111

Theory 27, 54, 56, 58, 116, 120, 174, 186, 193, 198–199

Thinking backwards 13

Thomas, Janice 207

Time 19, 20, 39, 56, 64, 67, 68, 69, 109, 110, 111, 113, 115, 122, 123, 126, 130, 137, 140, 169, 174, 175, 183, 184, 185, 187, 188, 192, 212, 213

Time performance 64, 67–96

Top down estimation 95

Top down planning 195

Tradeoff 117, 118, 135, 136, 156, 221

Transparency 20, 139, 140, 143, 194, 214

Triple bottom line 139
Trust 38, 56, 102, 110, 130, 151, 173,
        174, 175, 179, 180, 194, 197

Uncertainty 3, 4, 7–13, 17, 23, 28, 39–40,
        42, 50, 55, 56, 103, 128, 129, 136,
        172, 173, 174, 180, 191, 221
Uncertainty management strategies 12
    Adapt 12
    Detour 12
    Reorient 12
    Suppress 12

Unknown unknowns 3, 7, 10, 132

Value 3, 4, 28, 34, 40, 41, 43, 44, 45, 46,
        47, 56, 67, 115, 118, 137, 155,
        156, 207
Visibility 63
Vision 3, 39–40, 42, 44, 60, 61, 100,
        101, 145, 180, 188

Wicked problems 49–50, 53–4, 55

Yerkes-Dodson Principle 169–171

Advances in Project Management

Advances in Project Management provides short, state of play, guides to the main aspects of the new emerging applications including: maturity models, agile projects, extreme projects, Six Sigma and projects, human factors and leadership in projects, project governance, value management, virtual teams and project benefits.

Currently Published Titles

Project Ethics, Haukur Ingi Jonasson and Helgi Thor Ingason 978-1-4094-1096-6

Managing Project Uncertainty, David Cleden 978-0-566-08840-7

Managing Project Supply Chains, Ron Basu 978-1-4094-2515-1

Project-Oriented Leadership, Ralf Müller and J Rodney Turner 978-0-566-08923-7

Strategic Project Risk Appraisal and Management, Elaine Harris 978-0-566-08848-3

Spirituality and Project Management, Judi Neal and Alan Harpham 978-1-4094-0959-5

Sustainability in Project Management, Gilbert Silvius, Jasper van den Brink, Ron Schipper, Adri Köhler and Julia Planko 978-1-4094-3169-5

Second Order Project Management, Michael Cavanagh 978-1-4094-1094-2

Tame, Messy and Wicked Risk Leadership, David Hancock 978-0-566-09242-8

Reviews of the Series

MANAGING PROJECT UNCERTAINTY, DAVID CLEDEN

This is a must-read book for anyone involved in project management. The author's carefully crafted work meets all my '4Cs' review criteria. The book is clear, cogent, concise and complete...it is a brave author who essays to write about managing project uncertainty in a text extending to only 117 pages (soft-cover version). In my opinion, David Cleden succeeds brilliantly...For project managers this book, far from being a short-lived stress anodyne, will provide a confidence-boosting tonic. Project uncertainty? Bring it on, I say!

International Journal of Managing Projects in Business

Uncertainty is an inevitable aspect of most projects, but even the most proficient project manager struggles to successfully contain it. Many projects overrun and consume more funds than were originally budgeted, often leading to unplanned expense and outright programme failure. David examines how uncertainty occurs and provides management strategies that the user can put to immediate use on their own project work. He also provides a series of pre-emptive uncertainty and risk avoidance strategies that should be the cornerstone of any planning exercise for all personnel involved in project work.

I have been delivering both large and small projects and programmes in the public and private sector since 1989. I wish this book had been available when I began my career in project work. I strongly commend this book to all project professionals.

Lee Hendricks, Sales & Marketing Director,
SunGard Public Sector

The book under review is an excellent presentation of a comprehensive set of explorations about uncertainty (its recognition) in the context of projects. It does a good job of all along reinforcing the difference between risk (known unknowns) management and managing uncertainty (unknown unknowns – 'bolt from the blue'). The author lucidly presents a variety of frameworks/ models so that the reader easily grasps the varied forms in which uncertainty presents itself in the context of projects.

VISION – The Journal of Business Perspective (India)

Cleden will leave you with a sound understanding about the traits, tendencies, timing and tenacity of uncertainty in projects. He is also adept at identifying certain methods that try to contain the uncertainty, and why some prove more successful than others. Those who expect risk management to be the be-all, end-all for uncertainty solutions will be in for a rude awakening.

Brad Egeland, *Project Management Tips*

PROJECT-ORIENTED LEADERSHIP, RODNEY TURNER AND RALF MÜLLER

Müller and Turner have compiled a terrific 'ready-reckoner' that all project managers would benefit from reading and reflecting upon to challenge their performance. The authors have condensed considerable experience and research from a wide variety of professional disciplines, to provide a robust digest that highlights the significance of leadership capabilities for effective delivery of project outcomes. One of the big advantages of this book is the richness of the content and the natural flow of their argument throughout such a short book…Good advice, well explained and backed up with a body of evidence…I will be recommending the book to colleagues who are in project leader and manager roles and to students who are considering these as part of their development or career path.

Arthur Shelley, RMIT University, Melbourne, Australia,

International Journal of Managing Projects in Business

In a remarkably succinct 89 pages, Müller and Turner review an astonishing depth of evidence, supported by their own (published) research which challenges many of the commonly held assumptions not only about project management, but about what makes for successful leaders.

This book is clearly written more for the project-manager type personality than for the natural leader. Concision, evidence and analysis are the main characteristics of the writing style…it is massively authoritative, and so carefully written that a couple of hours spent in its 89 pages may pay huge dividends compared to the more expansive, easy reading style of other management books.

Mike Turner, Director of Communications for NHS Warwickshire

STRATEGIC PROJECT RISK APPRAISAL AND MANAGEMENT, ELAINE HARRIS

…Elaine Harris's volume is timely. In a world of books by 'instant experts' it's pleasing to read something by someone who clearly knows their onions, and has a passion for the subject…In summary, this is a thorough and engaging book.

Chris Morgan, Head of Business Assurance
for Select Plant Hire, Quality World

As soon as I met Elaine I realised that we both shared a passion to better understand the inherent risk in any project, be that capital investment, expansion capital or expansion of assets. What is seldom analysed are the components of knowledge necessary to make a good judgement, the impact of our own prejudices in relation to projects or for that matter the cultural elements within an organisation which impact upon the decision making process. Elaine created a system to break this down and give reasons and logic to both the process and the human interaction necessary to improve the chances of success. Adopting her recommendations will improve teamwork and outcomes for your company.

Edward Roderick Hon LLD, Former CEO Christian Salvesen Plc

TAME, MESSY AND WICKED RISK LEADERSHIP, DAVID HANCOCK

This book takes project risk management firmly onto a higher and wider plane. We thought we knew what project risk management was and what it could do. David Hancock shows us a great deal more of both. David Hancock has probably read more about risk management than almost anybody else, he has almost certainly thought about it as much as anybody else and he has quite certainly learnt from doing it on very difficult projects as much as anybody else. His book draws fully on all three components. For a book which tackles a complex subject with breadth, insight and novelty – its remarkable that it is also a really good read. I could go on!

Dr Martin Barnes CBE FREng, President,
The Association for Project Management

This compact and thought provoking description of risk management will be useful to anybody with responsibilities for projects, programmes or businesses. It hits the nail on the head in so many ways, for example by pointing out that risk management can easily drift into a check-list mindset, driven by the production of registers of numerous occurrences characterised by the Risk = Probablity x Consequence equation. David Hancock points out that real life is much more complicated, with the heart of the problem lying in people, so that real life resembles poker rather than roulette. He also points out that while the important thing is to solve the right problem, many real life issues cannot be readily described in a definitive statement of the problem. There are often interrelated individual problems with surrounding social issues and he describes these real life situations as 'Wicked Messes'. Unusual terminology, but definitely worth the read, as much for the overall problem description as for the recommended strategies for getting to grips with real life risk management. I have no hesitation in recommending this book.

Sir Robert Walmsley KCB FREng,
Chairman of the Board of the Major Projects Association

In highlighting the complexity of many of today's problems and defining them as tame, messy or wicked, David Hancock brings a new perspective to the risk issues that we currently face. He challenges risk managers, and particularly those involved in project risk management, to take a much broader approach to the assessment of risk and consider the social, political and behavioural dimensions of each problem, as well as the scientific and engineering aspects with which they are most comfortable. In this way, risks will be viewed more holistically and managed more effectively than at present.

Dr Lynn T Drennan, Chief Executive, Alarm,
the Public Risk Management Association

SUSTAINABILITY IN PROJECT MANAGEMENT, GILBERT SILVIUS, JASPER VAN DEN BRINK, RON SCHIPPER, ADRI KÖHLER AND JULIA PLANKO

Sustainability in Project Management thinking and techniques is still in its relatively early days. By the end of this decade it will probably be universal, ubiquitous, fully integrated and expected. This book will be a most valuable guide on this journey for all those interested in the future of projects and how they are managed in a world in peril.

Tom Taylor dashdot and vice-President of APM

Project Managers are faced with lots of intersections. The intersection of projects and risk, projects and people, projects and constraints... Sustainability in Projects and Project Management is a compelling, in-depth treatment of a most important intersection: the intersection of project management and sustainability. With detailed background building to practical checklists and a call to action, this book is a must-read for anyone interested in truly implementing sustainability, project manager or not.

Rich Maltzman, PMP, Co-Founder, EarthPM, LLC,
and co-author of *Green Project Management*,
Cleland Literature Award Winner of 2011

Great book! Based on a thorough review on existing relevant models and concepts the authors provide guidance for different stakeholders such as Project Managers and Project Office Managers to consider sustainability principles on projects. The book gets you started on sustainability in project context!

Martina Huemann, WU-Vienna University of Economics
and Business, Vienna Austria

While sustainability and green business have been around a while, this book is truly a 'call to action' to help the project manager, or for that matter, anyone, seize the day and understand sustainability from a project perspective. This book gives real and practical suggestions as to how to fill the sustainability/project gap within your organization. I particularly liked the relationship between sustainability and 'professionalism and ethics', a connection that needs to be kept in the forefront.

David Shirley, PMP, Co-Founder, EarthPM, LLC,
and co-author of *Green Project Management*,
Cleland Literature Award Winner of 2011

It is high time that quality corporate citizenship takes its place outside the corporate board room. This excellent work, which places the effort needed to secure sustainability for everything we do right where the rubber hits the road – our projects – has been long overdue. Thank you Gilbert, Jasper, Ron, Adri and Julia for doing just that! I salute you.

Jaycee Krüger, member of ISO/TC258
a technical committee for the creation of standards in Project,
Program and Portfolio Management, and chair of SABS/TC258,
the South African mirror committee of ISO/TC258

Sustainability is no passing fad. It is the moral obligation that we all face in ensuring the future of human generations to come. The need to show stewardship and act as sustainability change agents has never been greater. As project managers we are at the forefront of influencing the direction of our projects and our organisations. Sustainability in Project Management offers illuminating insights into the concept of sustainability and its application to project management. It is a must read for any modern project manager.

Dr Neveen Moussa, Project Manager, Adjunct Professor
of Project Management and past president of the Australian
Institute of Project Management

About the Editor

Professor Darren Dalcher is founder and Director of the National Centre for Project Management, a Professor of Project Management at the University of Hertfordshire and Visiting Professor of Computer Science at the University of Iceland.

Following industrial and consultancy experience in managing IT projects, Professor Dalcher gained his PhD from King's College, University of London. In 1992, he founded and chaired of the Forensics Working Group of the IEEE Technical Committee on the Engineering of Computer-Based Systems, an international group of academic and industrial participants formed to share information and develop expertise in project and system failure and recovery.

He is active in numerous international committees, standards bodies, steering groups, and editorial boards. He is heavily involved in organising international conferences, and has delivered many international keynote addresses and tutorials. He has written over 150 refereed papers and book chapters on project management and software engineering. He is Editor-in-Chief of the *International Journal of Software Maintenance and Evolution*, and of the *Journal of Software: Evolution and Process*. He is the editor of a major new book series, Advances in Project Management, published by Gower Publishing which synthesises leading edge knowledge, skills, insights and reflections in project and programme management and of a new companion series, Fundamentals of Project Management, which provides the essential grounding in key areas of project management.

He has built a reputation as leader and innovator in the area of practice-based education and reflection in project management and has worked with many major industrial, commercial and charitable organisations and government bodies. In 2008 he was named by the Association for Project Management as one of the top 10 influential experts in project management and has also been voted *Project Magazine's* Academic of the Year for his contribution in 'integrating and weaving academic work with practice'. He has been chairman of the APM Project Management Conference since 2009, setting consecutive attendance records and bringing together the most influential speakers.

He received international recognition in 2009 with appointment as a member of the PMForum International Academic Advisory Council, which features leading academics from some of the world's top universities and academic institutions. The Council showcases accomplished researchers, influential educators shaping the next generation of project managers and recognised authorities on modern project management. In October 2011 he was awarded a prestigious Honorary Fellowship from the Association for Project Management for outstanding contribution to project management.

He has delivered lectures and courses in many international institutions, including King's College London, Cranfield Business School, ESC Lille, Iceland University, University of Southern Denmark, and George Washington University. His research interests include project success and failure; maturity and capability; ethics; process improvement; agile project management; systems and software engineering; project benchmarking; risk management; decision making; chaos and complexity; project leadership; change management; knowledge management; evidence-based and reflective practice.

Professor Dalcher is an Honorary Fellow of the Association for Project Management, a Chartered Fellow of the British Computer Society, a Fellow of the Chartered Management Institute, and the Royal Society of Arts, and a Member of the Project Management Institute, the Academy of Management, the Institute for Electrical and Electronics Engineers, and the Association for Computing Machinery. He is a Chartered IT Practitioner. He is a Member of the PMI Advisory Board responsible for the prestigious David I. Cleland Project Management Award; of the APM Group Ethics and Standards Governance Board, and, until recently; of the APM Professional Development Board. He is a member of the OGC's International Reference Group for Managing Successful Programmes; and Academic and Editorial Advisory Council Member for *PM World Journal*, for which he also writes a regular column featuring advances in research and practice in project management.

National Centre for Project Management
University of Hertfordshire
MacLaurin Building
4 Bishops Square
Hatfield, Herts, AL10 9NE
Email: ncpm@herts.ac.uk